Penguin Masterstudies

George Eliot

The Mill on the Floss

Roger Ebbatson

Advisory Editors: Stephen Coote and Bryan Loughrey

Penguin Books

Penguin Books Ltd, Harmondsworth, Middlesex, England
Viking Penguin Inc., 40 West 23rd Street, New York, New York 10010, U.S.A.
Penguin Books Australia Ltd, Ringwood, Victoria, Australia
Penguin Books Canada Ltd, 2801 John Street, Markham, Ontario, Canada L3R 1B4
Penguin Books (N.Z.) Ltd, 182–190 Wairau Road, Auckland 10, New Zealand

First published 1985

Made and printed in Great Britain by
Richard Clay (The Chaucer Press) Ltd, Bungay, Suffolk
Filmset in 9/11 pt Monophoto Times by
Northumberland Press Ltd, Gateshead, Tyne and Wear

Contents

1. Biographical Sketch   9
2. The Composition of the Novel   11
3. The Economic Background   12
4. Table of Relationships   14
5. The Background of Ideas   16
6. General Plot Summary   22
7. Detailed Plot Summary and Chronology   24
8. Analysis: 35
    The Narrative Voice   35
    Realism   39
    Character in the Novel   41
    Society and the Individual   53
    The Feminist Perspective   62
    The Crisis   67
    The Tragic Ending   70
    Select Bibliography   74

Preface

It has been well said that great literature possesses 'the power to show us alternative ways of experiencing the world'. George Eliot would have agreed, and in *The Mill on the Floss* she creates a rich and various world which may lie both within and without our own experience. This imaginative world lies within in so far as any novel tracing the passage from childhood to adulthood calls upon the experience of every reader. It lies without, in the triumphant ability of the novel to register, record and celebrate provincial ways of life which are now becoming lost to us.

I should like to record my gratitude to my colleagues Roger Alma and Catherine Neale for their valuable advice in the preparation of this study.

All page references to the novel are to the Penguin English Library edition edited by A. S. Byatt (Penguin Books, 1979). Other quotations are from *Essays of George Eliot*, edited by Thomas Pinney (Routledge and Kegan Paul, 1963).

Roger Ebbatson

1. Biographical Sketch

George Eliot was born Mary Ann Evans on 22 November 1819. Her father was Robert Evans, overseer to the Arbury Hall estate in Warwickshire from 1806, a man of great physical strength and personal integrity. He had begun life as a carpenter, but his wide practical knowledge had secured him the surveyorship. His first wife died in 1809, and in 1813 he married Christiana Pearson, the daughter of a well-established yeoman. Christiana had three sisters who seem to have provided models for the Dodsons. Like them they revered:

whatever was customary and respectable: it was necessary to be baptised, else one could not be buried in the churchyard, and to take the sacrament before death as a security against more dimly understood perils; but it was of equal necessity to have the proper pall-bearers and well-cured hams at one's funeral, and to leave an unimpeachable will.   (p. 364)

There had been two children from the first marriage, Robert (1802) and Frances (1805); Christiana gave birth to Chrissey (1814), Isaac (1816) and Mary Ann (1819), all of whom were born at South Farm, Arbury. After Mary Ann's birth the family moved to a farmhouse at Griff, a location which, with its adjacent pool, may have furnished a model for some of the features of Dorlcote Mill. Mary Ann was rather a favourite child with her father, and she often accompanied him on his rounds. Mr Evans was to be portrayed admiringly in George Eliot's fictional works as Adam Bede and Caleb Garth, and somewhat more critically as Mr Tulliver. The emotional pattern of Mary Ann's dependence upon a stronger male seems to have begun at this time. The other dominant relationship of her childhood was with her brother Isaac, whom she followed about 'puppy-like' on his fishing expeditions and other adventures. Isaac provided Mary Ann with what her husband John Cross was to describe as her 'absolute need of some one person who should be all in all to her, and to whom she should be all in all'. A cancelled passage of *The Mill on the Floss* interestingly portrays Maggie fantasizing about the character of her brother and transforming him into a person 'never angry with her if she forgot anything', one who loved her 'more, even than she loved him, so that he would always want to have her with him and be afraid of vexing her'. In 1824 the pair were separated, as Isaac was sent off to boarding school, and in 1828 Mary Ann was sent to school at Nuneaton. Here she came under the tutelage of Maria Lewis, who was a crucial figure in her development. Miss Lewis was of a firmly evangelical persuasion, and placed great stress on self-denial and renunciation. At around the age of fifteen, Mary Ann underwent the type of 'conversion' which Maggie experiences in the novel after reading Thomas à Kempis. After her mother's death, and Isaac's marriage, Mary Ann and her father moved in 1841 closer to Coventry. The town was a centre of radical thought, and, under the intellectual guidance of her friends the Brays and Hennells, Mary Ann came to discard her evangelical faith to the extent that in 1842 she refused to accompany her father to church. She now clung to 'the truth of feeling as the only universal bond of union'. Although she later compromised, this refusal led to a serious breach with her father which was never truly healed up to the time of his death in 1849.

Mary Ann had worked diligently at her own education in languages and philosophy, and in 1844 she undertook the major task of translating D. F. Strauss's *Life of Jesus*, part of the so-called New Criticism which was approaching Biblical material in a rationalist spirit. This work brought her into touch with some of the leading intellectuals of mid-Victorian England, such as Herbert Spencer and Frederic Harrison, and in 1852 Mary Ann moved to London to become assistant editor of John Chapman's free-thinking *Westminster Review*. Around this time she first met the critic and naturalist G. H. Lewes. Lewes was a short, physically unattractive man of great dynamism and intellectual curiosity. In 1854 Mary Ann and Lewes left for Germany in the guise of man and wife, despite the fact that Lewes was already married. This action provoked scandal in respectable circles, and on their return to England Mary Ann was compelled to lead a life of relative solitude. Under Lewes's encouragement, Mary Ann began to experiment with fiction, and composed a series of realistic provincial *Scenes of Clerical Life* in 1856. Over the subsequent period of twenty years she published her major novels under the pseudonym 'George Eliot', prompted and inspired by Lewes.

The Mill on the Floss (1860) was the third of these fictional works, and followed upon her greatest popular success, *Adam Bede* (1859). *Middlemarch* (1872), now regarded as her most important novel, was followed, in 1876, by *Daniel Deronda*. Two years later, however, Lewes died and her novel-writing career came to an end. In 1880 she married a younger man, J. W. Cross, and re-established the contact with her brother Isaac which had been broken off by her extra-marital union with Lewes. Mary Ann died in London on 22 December 1880.

2. The Composition of the Novel

George Eliot first referred to her new novel in January 1859, when she recorded how she and Lewes visited London 'and looked in the Annual Register for cases of inundation'. In her Commonplace Book the author carefully noted down several accounts of the floods of the 1770s in the north of England, and one of a flood in Coventry. Details from these were to be incorporated into the final pages of her novel, and it is clear from these preparatory studies that the flood was not an afterthought. The period of composition of *The Mill on the Floss* was a worrying one for George Eliot because of the rift with her brother Isaac over her cohabitation with Lewes, and it was further saddened by the death of her sister Chrissey. Thus family matters were very much on her mind during the process of composition of the childhood sections. In the summer of 1859, when the story was well under way, George Eliot and Lewes investigated the workings of a mill near Weymouth in Dorset. In September they made a more significant journey to look at the Trent valley around Gainsborough in Lincolnshire, and it was this town which was to provide the model for St Ogg's. The first two volumes of *The Mill on the Floss* were completed by January 1860. Volume three was written more rapidly, being completed in March 1860. The first edition, comprising three volumes, was published by Blackwood's on 4 April 1860, at a cost to the readership of 31s. 6d. It was republished in other editions a further four times during the author's lifetime.

3. The Economic Background

The first two volumes are set substantially in the Warwickshire country-side of George Eliot's childhood memory. The action centres upon her reminiscences of Griff House at Chilvers Coton. The Red Deeps recall the Griff Hollows, and Arbury Mill close to Griff provided a model for Dorlcote Mill. George Eliot, however, found it necessary to transfer the action to the more substantial River Trent in Lincolnshire in order to account for the final catastrophe, although confusingly the dialect often remains closer to that of her native county. Gainsborough lent some of its features to the fictional St Ogg's, not only in its position in the Trent valley, with its wharves and river trade, but also in the medieval Old Hall, which, combined with features of St Mary's Hall in Coventry, served as the venue for the climactic charity bazaar in the novel. Other local places which may be identified include Lindum, the Roman name for Lincoln, Luckreth, which may be Stockwith, on the Trent, Tofton, which may be Morton, where George Eliot stayed, and Mudport, which appears to be Hull on the Humber estuary.

Despite George Eliot's somewhat cursory visit to Lincolnshire she is able to reproduce in fictional form elements of the economic changes of the period and the region quite accurately. Lincolnshire, like other rural counties, was ceasing in the early nineteenth century to be solely agricultural. Instead, farming, industry and commerce combined as factors of change, to the extent that the period 1740–1870 saw a population increase of 60 per cent in the Trent valley. The major stimulus of change came from the development of Trent-side shipping, which was not to be superseded in importance until the opening of the railway from Sheffield to Grimsby in 1847, after the period of the novel's action. During this period, agriculture in the Trent lowlands improved through the intro-duction of 'warping' – the practice of controlling and releasing river water at will (a practice so annoying to Mr Tulliver). This process created rich new soil on the surrounding land, and was usually undertaken through the initiative of some enterprising landowner (Mr Pivart in the novel). A historian of the area notes the difficulties of such arrangements further downstream, but adds that 'the participation of others was not difficult to arrange if satisfactory articles of agreement were drawn up' – the very thing that Mr Tulliver will not countenance. In some Trent villages great fortunes were amassed very rapidly in the early part of the nineteenth century. As the same historian observes, 'There is no doubt that enclosure and the imports which made it possible roused ambitions ... The fresh opportunities, suddenly opened up, brought into action stores of human energy never previously tapped.' The nature of these openings and their exploitation is accurately mirrored in the bustling commercial life of St Ogg's, and especially in the deployment of capital and property by Mr Deane and Mr Wakem. Mr Tulliver seems, in this respect, to stand against the spirit of the times, whereas even Tom's speculations with Bob Jakin neatly reflect the new and invigorating thrust of entrepreneurial capitalism. Mr Tulliver finds himself enmeshed by this new spirit. The mill is central to his emotional life, and, as he tells Luke, 'I should go off my head in a new place' (p. 353). The process of change in town and country is what Mr Tulliver obdurately sets his face against. The economics of the novel, and particularly the new idea of putting money to *use*, help towards creating the tragic dilemma of Tulliver's position.

The economics of Tulliver's problems need to be very clearly understood by the reader. Overall, he appears to owe some £5,000, a large amount of money at that time. Not all of his expenses are clearly defined, but we may outline quite positively most of the income and outgoings: on the debit side there is £300 lent to Mrs Moss; £100 for Tom's education; £2,000 mortgage on the land, which Fawley transfers to Wakem; £50 owed to Luke; £500 owed to Mrs Glegg, repaid by Tulliver at the cost of mortgaging the household; £250 suretyship for Mr Riley, which Tulliver loses; living expenses, not specified; a bank loan and other debts not detailed; lawsuit costs against Pivart. Against this crushing weight of debt and litigation we may set the undefined income from the mill itself. This kind of analysis helps us to understand how it is that Mr Tulliver's stand against the new economic forces turns out so disastrously for him, and how counterproductive is the influence of his wife, both in strengthening his determination to repay Mrs Glegg, and in her appeal to Wakem over the sale of the mill. Tulliver, that is to say, is a man trapped not only by the laws of his own character, but also by the inexorable laws of business which distinguish St Ogg's from the rural peace of Dorlcote Mill. These laws are part of a new ethos of survival. What the novel powerfully tends to question is whether the fittest to survive are ethically the best.

4. Table of Relationships

Tullivers:

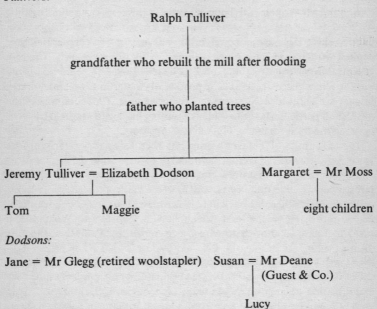

Ralph Tulliver
|
grandfather who rebuilt the mill after flooding
|
father who planted trees
|

Jeremy Tulliver = Elizabeth Dodson   Margaret = Mr Moss

Tom   Maggie   eight children

Dodsons:

Jane = Mr Glegg (retired woolstapler)   Susan = Mr Deane
                                      (Guest & Co.)

Lucy

Sophie = Mr Pullet   Elizabeth = Jeremy Tulliver
(retired farmer)

Tom   Maggie

Other characters:
Luke Moggs, head miller
Bob Jakin, packman
Mr Riley, auctioneer
Mr Gore, lawyer
Mr Pivart, farmer
Mr Stelling, clergyman and schoolmaster
Mr Wakem
Philip Wakem
Stephen Guest
Dr Kenn, clergyman

5. The Background of Ideas

George Eliot early in her career underwent a typically Victorian crisis of faith, and was led through this experience to transfer the spiritual values upheld by Christianity to the ordinary daily experience of humanity. She was most thoroughly educated in the techniques and modes of rationalism and the methods of the 'higher criticism' of the Bible and other documents. Her relationships with such writers as Herbert Spencer, Frederic Harrison and Lewes himself gave her an impressive grounding in the procedures of experimental science and deductive philosophy. Her reading of Comte, Feuerbach and others was of crucial significance in revealing a progressive world-view of history and human life. George Eliot came to believe, through immersing herself in such reading, in a 'religion of humanity' which was supported and endorsed by the imaginative experience of the individual. The fresh perspectives created by mid-Victorian developments in geology, biology and anthropology permitted the reconciliation of morality based upon freedom of the will with scientific determinism. For George Eliot the essence of rationalism was the reduction of all phenomena to a position within the realm of established law, and this led her to the study of human development and what she termed 'the inexorable law of consequence'. Darwin's *The Origin of Species* was published in 1859, just as she began work on *The Mill on the Floss*. She was receptive to his thesis, and often traces a type of moral evolution in her novels. Within the narrative limits of *The Mill on the Floss*, for instance, there is a clear evolutionary advance between the Dodsons and the aspirations of Maggie and Philip. Yet George Eliot was convinced that the Darwinian thesis produced in her 'a feeble impression compared with the mystery that lies under the processes'. This 'mystery' perhaps derives from her sense of the pieties of childhood, home and family life. In her writing, limitations on human nature and the human condition provide a foundation within which she can paradoxically assert the purpose and dignity of human life. The novel as she inherited it from Scott, Fielding, Dickens and Mrs Gaskell provided her with a form in which she could describe individuals acting in society and in relation to nature, just as Hardy was to do later. As she saw it, the value of fiction lay in its capacity to extend the sympathies of the reader: 'Art is the nearest thing to life; it is a mode of amplifying experience and extending our contact with our fellow-men beyond the bounds of our personal lot'

(*Essays*, p. 271). It has sometimes been said that this view makes her novels heavily 'philosophical'; Henry James, for example, asserted that 'the philosophic door is always open, on her stage, and we are aware that the somewhat cooling draught of ethical purpose draws across it'. Although there is a weight of generalization in the novel, the richness and depth of the felt life always checks this 'ethical purpose' and turns it into art.

The picture painted of St Ogg's is of a society evolving, as George Eliot had indicated in something she wrote three years before starting work on the novel:

> What has grown up historically can only die out historically, by the gradual operation of necessary laws. The external conditions which society has inherited from the past are but the manifestation of inherited internal conditions and the external are related to each other as the organism and its medium, and development can take place only by the gradual ... development of both. (*Essays*, p. 287)

George Eliot believes in progress, and shows its operations in St Ogg's. She also clings to the past. Many of her novels are set in recent history, and enable her to explore the values of tradition and family. Maggie is caught between her unfulfilled aspirations and her piety towards the past. George Eliot had spoken in *Adam Bede* of a nature which:

> knits us together by bone and muscle, and divides us by a subtler web of our brains; blends yearning and repulsion; and ties us by our tent-strings to the beings that jar us at every moment.

If the events in her world are determined, men yet remain somehow responsible for their actions: Tulliver is caught by the forces of economic change, but is ultimately responsible for his own downfall. The image of the web is central for George Eliot, since it shows the universe to be a network of interdependent parts. A very simple demonstration of this principle would be Pivart's action in stopping the flow of river water which affects Tulliver's trade. This is a crude model for all the human relations in the novel, and it is the network of relationships from which Maggie finally, and tragically, cuts herself off. George Eliot's vision of this society is profoundly democratic. She does not deal with elevated personages, since, as she declares in the novel, 'there is nothing petty to the mind that has a large vision of relations'. It is through Wordsworthian 'unremembered acts' that the world progresses, or, as it is phrased in *Middlemarch*, 'The growing good of the world is partly dependent on unhistoric acts.' The emphasis on action is at the nub of George Eliot's belief, and at the heart of the problem she has set herself to solve, that of relating a deterministic view of history to a belief in the individual will. There is an ambiguity in the relations between external forces and inner desires which constantly surfaces in the creation of Maggie. Maggie is not, as Hardy wrote of Tess, a 'victim': she is capable of making her character through her own decisions or (as in the boating episode) indecisions. She strives, after floating away with Stephen, to renounce her own desires for what she conceives as nobler ends, and returns to the harsh judgement of St Ogg's. In such crises George Eliot is mobilizing and dramatizing her sense of the intertwining elements of determinism and free will in the society. Maggie's faith in her childhood ties clashes with the imaginative hunger to which Philip Wakem and Stephen Guest differently appeal. Maggie is truly a romantic spirit, and her ardent inner nature inevitably collides with an oppressive outer world dominated by people such as the 'emmet-like Dodsons'. Tom's inability to share this romantic feeling enables him to persevere at his self-denying goals. Although the brother and sister grow apart through the decisive influence of inner development and outer fact, George Eliot's romantic sensibility dictated that they should be finally reconciled. This controversial decision marks most dramatically in this particular novel a perennial problem of belief for George Eliot. In the final analysis, determinism of place and character are overcome by some private myth of reconciliation.

In a famous conversation with a Cambridge don, George Eliot discussed the terms 'God, Immortality, and Duty'. She declared to her hearer 'how inconceivable was the *first*, how unbelievable the *second*, and yet how peremptory and absolute the *third*'. This declaration, it might be suggested, encompasses her own intellectual development, since she began with the deity, as an evangelical believer, and in her maturity believed only in the operation of rationalist ethics. Yet the rationalist discourse and tradition to which she exposed herself on the *Westminster Review*, and in her translations of Strauss and Feuerbach, became modified, in her early fiction, by her strong feelings about childhood and family pieties. What distinguishes man from the animals, she suggests in *The Mill on the Floss*, is 'the striving after something better and better in our surroundings' (p. 222), but this note of striving is counteracted throughout her work by the way the affections have a 'trick of twining round those old inferior things' (ibid.); the 'loves and sanctities' of our life, that is to say, possess 'deep immovable roots in memory' (ibid.). God is replaced by humanity in George Eliot's pantheon, religious faith by sympathy and human feeling. She did not, however, reject religion outright. On the contrary, she valued 'that which is essentially human in all forms of belief', and sought 'the lasting meaning that lies in all religious doctrine'.

There is in her novels a feeling that general dogma is deceptive, 'if unchecked by the deep-seated habit of direct fellow-feeling with individual fellow-men', as she expresses it in *Middlemarch*. Human progress in moral terms is to be measured 'by the degree in which we sympathise with individual suffering and individual joy', and it is precisely this absence of suffering which mars the moral development of Tom Tulliver, or, in a wider sense, the Dodsons as a group. The aim of fiction, in the view of George Eliot, is to evoke and extend this feeling of understanding and empathy, 'to call forth tolerant judgement, pity and sympathy'. George Eliot saw herself to some degree as a sage. Her aim through literature was to urge 'fellowship between man and man' by realistic portrayals of obscure and often mediocre personages. She urges upon the reader of *Adam Bede* that 'it is these more or less ugly, stupid, inconsistent people whose movements of goodness you should be able to admire'. Her powerful and consistently held conviction of the lovable nature of common humanity had come about, she claimed, 'by living a great deal among people more or less commonplace or vulgar'. The 'message' she seeks to transmit, however, would be weak and thin if it were not cast through the realist mode of fiction; as she herself remarked, 'ideas are often poor ghosts'. The novels are to be seen, then, as fictions which give the reader examples of lives which may be claimed to possess typicality. They are mainly set in the recent past, and give a sense of gradual historical change. The background to *The Mill on the Floss*, for instance, is an expansion of material progress which buoys up entrepreneurs like Deane and Wakem. Within the analysis of these changes, George Eliot pays close attention to the subtle interactions between town and country, and dramatizes these through the differing ranks and occupations of characters who have a living to earn in this developing society. There are subtle discriminations, therefore, within the social strata of St Ogg's: Deane, for example, was originally thought a poorer marital catch than Pullet, but the tide of economic opportunity carries him upwards financially and socially. George Eliot marshals her evidence with minute fidelity to truth, and demonstrates her range with the wide variety of character types from Bob Jakin up to Stephen Guest. The most significant figures historically speaking may be those who are moving upwards, such as Deane and Wakem, and those who are falling, such as Tulliver and Moss. It is an important comment upon the Dodsons that they appear to be static at a time of change. The layered complexities of such a treatment are finely summarized in *Middlemarch*, where the narrator remarks upon the 'slow preparation of effects from one life to another', and proceeds to analyse the way that the 'old provincial society' shows evidence not only of 'striking downfalls' like Tulliver's, 'but also those less marked vicissitudes which are constantly shifting the boundaries of social intercourse, and begetting new consciousness of interdependence'. Such an analysis is bound to stress determinism in the social structure, and this emphasis is heightened by the role of family life in the novels. Children will reproduce parental characteristics, but in modified form, and kinship is often experienced as a highly determining factor, as it is for Tom and Maggie.

A fiction which stresses cause and effect necessarily focuses upon long spans of time, and typically excludes the violent and melodramatic incidents cultivated by Dickens and other writers of the period. George Eliot wished to concentrate upon the gradual unfolding of character and causation, and it may be the break in that unfolding which leads some critics to baulk at the flood scene that drowns Tom and Maggie. The flood there denotes the arbitrary ending of what had seemed natural processes of growth. Indeed, growth and maturation are crucial elements in George Eliot's vision of life, and centre upon moral choice and awareness dramatized through characters who must act and suffer. In her approach to character we may discern several different but coherent techniques. There are, for instance, characters who may be read as representing a type, such as Bob Jakin or the Dodsons; there are characters who exemplify human beings caught within the laws of change, such as Tulliver or Deane; there are characters who embody authorial wisdom, such as Dr Kenn; and there are the central protagonists who learn and evolve, like Maggie. Maggie Tulliver, it is said, needs 'some explanation of this hard, real life ... some key that would enable her to understand' (p. 379). In a sense the entire novel is a record of that search for her destiny, for meaning. The image of the river, 'full and rapid' in its course, but leading to 'the same final home', embodies the sense of human life as moving onwards in a wider movement of events of which no one character can command an overview. Human change is allied, in George Eliot, to natural processes, and the development of moral awareness is an evolving one. She wrote in *Adam Bede* that human feeling 'like the mighty rivers that bless the earth ... flows with resistless force and brings beauty with it'. That is a crucial and abiding image. Realist fiction deals with the acts of individuals in time, and thus may be read as a kind of history. Certainly in the nineteenth century the novel became particularly engaged with historical processes. George Eliot said that she had 'arrived at a faith in the past but not at faith in the future'. This faith enabled her to construct her meticulous analyses of cause and effect within a historical continuum which transcends the fate of the individual caught up in it, and yet does not undervalue or dismiss that personal effort and struggle:

What we call illusions are often, in truth, a wider vision of past and present realities – a willing movement of a man's soul with the larger sweep of the world's forces – a movement towards a more assured end than the chances of a single life.   (*Felix Holt*)

6. General Plot Summary

The author dreams of Dorlcote Mill as it was thirty years ago. Inside the mill Mr and Mrs Tulliver are discussing how to educate their son Tom. Their daughter Maggie is cleverer and more passionate by nature, but she is devoted to her brother. The early chapters show how dependent Maggie feels upon Tom for her happiness. The opposition between the attitudes to life of the Tullivers and Dodsons is carefully dramatized. Mr Tulliver, a likeable and warmhearted man, is sadly ignorant of the ways of the world. Tom is sent to be educated in the classical style wholly unsuited to his temperament and opportunities. A family quarrel leads Mr Tulliver to vow to repay some money he owes to his sister-in-law, Mrs Glegg. Maggie's frequent unhappiness at home is dramatically presented in such episodes as cutting off her own hair, pushing Lucy into the mud, and running away to the gypsies. She twice visits Tom at his school, and on the second occasion meets Philip Wakem, the sensitive and crippled son of Lawyer Wakem, Mr Tulliver's prime enemy. Maggie pities Philip, and grows to like him a good deal. She is herself sent off to school with her cousin Lucy, but when she is thirteen is summoned home by her father's serious illness. Mr Tulliver has lost his lawsuit and been made bankrupt. At the age of sixteen Tom leaves school and tries to take over the running of affairs. While the family rallies round, Maggie is aware of their censorious attitude to her beloved father. Tom is now employed by his uncle, Mr Deane, at Guest and Co. in St Ogg's. The plan for Guest and Co. to buy the mill and retain Mr Tulliver as manager is baulked by Mrs Tulliver's hapless intervention with Mr Wakem, an act which puts into the lawyer's mind the idea of buying the mill himself in order to gain revenge on Tulliver. When Mr Tulliver recovers, he recognizes that he has no choice but to work for Wakem, and the family enter into a difficult period of subsistence living. Maggie feels particularly lonely and neglected, but gains spiritual strength from a reading of Thomas à Kempis's *The Imitation of Christ*. This leads her into a life of self-denial and acceptance of pain. Maggie, now seventeen, meets Philip once again, and goes on with clandestine meetings over a period of a year or more. Philip, who is in love with Maggie, holds out to her a world of art and culture which she has been starved of, but Tom discovers the fact of their meetings and in a cruel interview insults Philip and compels Maggie to end the relationship. Tom has been working devotedly for Guest and Co., and has also made money in a trading venture with Bob Jakin which enables him to pay off the family debts. After the creditors have been paid, Mr Tulliver encounters Wakem and attacks him on the road. The miller collapses in the melee, and dies the following day. After the death of her father, Maggie goes off to become a governess, and we next meet her at the age of nineteen when she has come on a prolonged visit to Lucy. Here she meets Stephen Guest, Lucy's suitor. The two are attracted to one another. Lucy wishes Philip to continue his visits to the house, and Tom ungraciously agrees to Maggie's seeing him again. Although Tom is now only twenty-three, he is made a partner in Guest and Co. because of his business acumen. He now plans to buy the mill for the firm and live there himself. Maggie is meanwhile enjoying a period of leisured culture, but is increasingly aware of her feelings for Stephen. Lucy is unaware of what is happening, but Philip begins to suspect the truth. Stephen makes his emotions known to Maggie, who is angry. She visits her aunt, Mrs Moss, but Stephen follows her and declares his love, and Maggie now reciprocates. The two continue to see one another in St Ogg's, believing that they will soon be parted. An expedition planned by Lucy goes awry when Philip is unable to row Maggie down the river because of the illness brought on by his jealousy. Stephen takes her instead, and without Maggie's knowledge deliberately allows their boat to drift past their place of rendezvous with Lucy. Stephen tries to persuade Maggie to elope with him, but she refuses because of her ties with Philip and Lucy. She returns alone to St Ogg's, but Tom, now installed again at the mill, disowns her. She and her mother move into Bob Jakin's house. She is befriended by the mature and kindly clergyman Dr Kenn, but ostracized by the polite society of St Ogg's. Both Philip and Lucy are kind and forgiving. She receives a letter from Stephen begging her to marry him, and while she seeks the strength to reject him the flood water enters the room. Maggie takes a boat and rescues Tom who is alone at the mill. They are reconciled and sail on in search of Lucy. The boat is sunk by floating debris and they die in one another's arms. Five years later we are shown that Stephen and Philip still visit the grave; as the years go by Lucy and Stephen will finally marry.

7. Detailed Plot Summary and Chronology

The novel spans the period from February 1829 to September 1839.

Book I

The action takes place between February 1829 and August 1829.

Chapter 1, *pp. 53–5*

The narrator sets the scene, describing St Ogg's, the river and the surrounding countryside. Dorlcote Mill is described, and the narrator notes the evidences of flooding in earlier days. A little girl watches the mill-wheel. The narrator now promises to go back into the past and recount the conversation between Mr and Mrs Tulliver.

Chapter 2, *pp. 56–62*

The Tullivers are discussing Tom's education. Mr Tulliver is ambitious for his son, while Mrs Tulliver is concerned only for his well-being. Tulliver decides to consult the local auctioneer on the question of a school for Tom. When the conversation turns to Maggie, it becomes clear that the Tullivers' daughter is a naughty, clever and wayward nine-year-old.

Chapter 3, *pp. 63–77*

The consultation with Mr Riley. Maggie is given a chance to show off her cleverness to the auctioneer, but he does not approve. Mr Riley recommends a clergyman as schoolmaster for Tom, but his motives in this are confused.

Chapter 4, *pp. 78–83*

Maggie is not allowed to go with her father to collect Tom from school. She takes out her anger on her old wooden doll. Later her spirits rise, and she takes the dog for a walk, but is reminded by Luke, her father's workman, that she has neglected Tom's rabbits and they have died. Luke invites her to his cottage to console her.

Chapter 5, *pp. 84–94*

Maggie is delighted to see Tom again, but her brother is incensed by the death of the rabbits. After retreating to the attic, Maggie is forgiven, and the pair enjoy a fishing trip together.

Chapter 6, *pp. 95–107*

A family gathering is being arranged to discuss Tom's future. The characteristics of the Dodson clan are fully analysed. Maggie is unhappy because Tom has gone on a jaunt with the disreputable Bob Jakin.

Chapter 7, *pp. 108–33*

The family gathers, and converses about illness, clothes and property. Because much is made of Lucy Deane's conventional prettiness, Maggie goes off and cuts her hair, much to the alarm of the company. The meeting ends in a row between Mr Tulliver and Mrs Glegg, to whom he owes money.

Chapter 8, *pp. 134–44*

Mrs Glegg now threatens reprisals by demanding repayment of the £500 which Mr Tulliver owes to her. This makes Tulliver determined to call in the £300 he has lent out to his sister and her unsuccessful farming husband. But when he visits the Mosses, sees their poverty, and thinks about Maggie's future, he changes his mind.

Chapter 9, *pp. 145 60*

Mrs Tulliver takes Maggie, Tom and Lucy on a visit to her sister, Mrs Pullet. Maggie feels jealous of Tom's friendship with Lucy. Mrs Pullet proudly displays her new bonnet, and Mrs Tulliver appeals to her to intervene in the dispute between her husband and Mrs Glegg.

Chapter 10, *pp. 161–7*

Lucy enters covered in dirt. She has been pushed into the mud by the jealous Maggie.

Chapter 11, *pp. 168–80*

Maggie is so unhappy she runs away to become queen of the gypsies. She is astonished and terrified by their threatening behaviour, however, and is retrieved by her father.

Chapter 12, *pp. 181–94*

A description of the history of St Ogg's is followed by an analysis of the marriage of Mr and Mrs Glegg. The latter decides not to press for the return of the £500.

Chapter 13, *pp. 195–8*

Just as Mrs Glegg is informing Mrs Pullet of her decision about the loan, she receives a letter from Mr Tulliver promising to repay the money in a month.

Book II

Tom's period at King's Lorton appears to extend from August 1829 to November 1832. Maggie's visits occur in October 1829 and spring 1830. There is some confusion over ages, but it seems that when Tom and Philip Wakem first meet they are respectively fourteen and fifteen.

Chapter 1, *pp. 201–22*

Tom's schoolmaster, Mr Stelling, is a conventionally minded clergyman. He inculcates Tom in the standard elements of gentlemanly education, founded in geometry and Latin. Tom fares badly, and is relieved by Maggie's visit. Maggie enjoys Latin, but her efforts are snubbed by Mr Stelling.

Chapter 2, *pp. 223–31*

Tom returns home for Christmas, but the family's happiness is over-shadowed by Mr Tulliver's irritable dabblings in legal matters. Maggie's father is annoyed by the interference of a neighbour in his water rights, and is convinced that his enemy Lawyer Wakem is behind it.

Chapter 3, *pp. 232–8*

On returning to school Tom discovers a new schoolfellow, Philip, the crippled son of Mr Wakem, his father's enemy. The new boy is sensitive and intellectually able, and the two form an uneasy friendship.

Chapter 4, *pp. 239–50*

Tom and Philip quarrel over sword drill.

Chapter 5, *pp. 251–6*

Maggie comes again, and Tom injures himself in his ostentatious sword practice.

Chapter 6, *pp. 257–62*

Tom and Philip are reconciled, and Maggie feels drawn to Philip because of his deformity. However, Tom and Philip gradually withdraw again into reserve and coolness.

Chapter 7, *pp. 263–70*

Maggie goes to school with Lucy, and loses touch with Philip Wakem. As Tom nears his final term, Maggie arrives to warn him that Mr Tulliver has lost the lawsuit, and is ill and bankrupt. They leave together, and the narrator reflects that their childhood is now at an end.

Book III

The action takes place during the winter of 1832–3.

Chapter 1, *pp. 273–9*

Mr Tulliver does not at first seem to recognize the scale and nature of his problems. When realization dawns he becomes seriously ill.

Chapter 2, *pp. 280–85*

Maggie and Tom arrive home to find the bailiff installed and Mrs Tulliver tearfully examining her household goods. Tom determines to get a job, while Maggie feels angrily that her brother and mother are unfairly blaming Mr Tulliver.

Chapter 3, *pp. 286–302*

A family council is called, and Tom's efforts are praised. Maggie sees that they all tend to blame her father. When Mrs Moss arrives the family insist that she should repay the £300, but Tom relates to them his father's determination never to seek repayment of the loan.

Chapter 4, *pp. 303–7*

The family search through legal papers, and Mr Tulliver seems to make a recovery, but his anger over Wakem causes a relapse. Tom decides to destroy the evidence of Mr Tulliver's loan to Mrs Moss, and to repay the £50 owing to Luke.

Chapter 5, *pp. 308–20*

Tom seeks an interview with his uncle, Mr Deane, who is disparaging about the utility of a classical education in business dealings. Tom takes out his pent-up anger on Maggie.

Chapter 6, *pp. 321–8*

The Tullivers' household goods are sold. Afterwards Bob Jakin offers the brother and sister a small gift of money.

Chapter 7, *pp. 329–41*

The date for the sale of Dorlcote Mill draws closer. Mr Deane is thinking over the possibility of Guest and Co. buying up the property and re-instating Mr Tulliver in the position of manager. Mrs Tulliver pays a secret visit to Mr Wakem and asks him not to bid against Mr Deane. This alerts Wakem to the sale, and to the possibility of acquiring the property as part of his revenge on Mr Tulliver.

Chapter 8, *pp. 342–50*

Mr Tulliver, on coming downstairs, sees for the first time how bereft the house is of furniture. Faced with the reality of his bankruptcy, he promises reluctantly to work for Wakem.

Chapter 9, *pp. 351–7*

Mr Tulliver finds the thought of being subordinate to Wakem difficult to stomach. He instructs Tom to write in the family Bible that he will work for the lawyer, but will never forgive him. Tom promises to seek vengeance.

Book IV

This mainly consists of authorial commentary. The scene in which Bob Jakin gives Maggie a collection of books takes place in the late spring of 1833.

Chapter 1, *pp. 361–6*

An extended analysis of the imaginative limitations of the Dodson way of life. Despite the manifest lack of spiritual values, the narrator finds worth in the Dodsons' devotion to honesty and application. The chapter also explains that the most ordinary life may contain the stuff of tragedy.

Chapter 2, *pp. 367–72*

Under the family's very straitened circumstances Mrs Tulliver becomes depressed, Tom silent, and Mr Tulliver ashamed. The family is now living at subsistence level.

Chapter 3, *pp. 373–88*

Bob Jakin's loan of some books allows Maggie to read in Thomas à Kempis's *The Imitation of Christ* of the dangers of self-love. This new perception leads her gradually to a greater humility and an acceptance of the family's reduced circumstances.

Book V

This book presents a rather confused time-scheme. Maggie and Philip first met at Lorton in 1830. They meet again in the Red Deeps in June 1836, although they say the period of their parting has been five years.

Tom begins to trade independently in August 1835. Philip Wakem declares his love for Maggie in April 1837, and Mr Tulliver dies that same spring.

Chapter 1, *pp. 391–404*

Maggie is intercepted in her lonely walks by Philip Wakem, who has painted a portrait of her. Although he clearly loves her, she can feel only friendship for him, but she reluctantly allows him to meet her again.

Chapter 2, *pp. 405–23*

Tom is now earning the admiration of the Dodsons by his application and industry, although repayment of the loan is a painfully slow business. Bob Jakin has thought up a scheme to invest in trade. Mr Tulliver is reluctant to risk their savings, but after a comic interlude Mrs Glegg is persuaded to finance the venture.

Chapter 3, *pp. 424–31*

Maggie tries to break off the relationship with Philip, but he argues that she is cutting herself off from life and culture. She eventually agrees to go on seeing him.

Chapter 4, *pp. 432–8*

After a gap of a year in the narrative, it appears that the two have been meeting regularly. Philip Wakem declares his love; Maggie feels that she would be making a noble sacrifice if she were to love him.

Chapter 5, *pp. 439–51*

Tom's suspicions are aroused by a stray remark of Mrs Pullet's. He accompanies Maggie to her meeting with Philip Wakem, insults him, and forces Maggie to give up her lover. Despite her anguish at the brutality of the scene, Maggie feels an obscure sense of relief at the enforced rupture.

Chapter 6, *pp. 452–7*

Tom tells his father that he is now able to pay off their debts as a result of his trading ventures with Bob Jakin. A meeting to pay off the creditors has been arranged.

Chapter 7, *pp. 458–65*

The triumphant moment of paying off the creditors is marred when Mr Tulliver meets Mr Wakem and attacks him. Maggie intervenes, and her father falls to the ground unconscious. Mr Tulliver dies the next morning, and Tom and Maggie are drawn together in their sorrow.

Book VI

Maggie arrives back in St Ogg's in May 1839. The journey down the river takes place in June, when she is nineteen, Tom twenty-three, Lucy eighteen, and Philip and Tom both twenty-five.

Chapter 1, *pp. 469–78*

Maggie has been away teaching for two years. Lucy is talking with Stephen Guest, son of the head of Guest and Co. Maggie is expected on a visit to Lucy, whose mother has died, and whose house is now looked after by Mrs Tulliver. Lucy and Stephen seem to be in love.

Chapter 2, *pp. 479–93*

Maggie returns, and meets Stephen Guest for the first time. Having been misled as to her appearance, Stephen is astonished at her beauty, but she does not respond to his polished courtesies.

Chapter 3, *pp. 494–8*

Lucy alarms Maggie by telling her that Philip Wakem will be calling the following day. Maggie now reveals her former relationship with Philip.

Chapter 4, *pp. 499–506*

Maggie goes to visit Tom, who is now living in the modest riverside house of Bob Jakin. Bob reveals that Tom may be in love with Lucy. Tom is displeased that Maggie wishes to renew her acquaintance with Philip Wakem, but they part affectionately.

Chapter 5, *pp. 507–11*

Mr Deane offers Tom a partnership in Guest and Co. Tom hopes the firm
will buy Dorlcote Mill and place him there as manager.

Chapter 6, *pp. 512–23*

Maggie and Stephen Guest enjoy one another's company, and they walk
in the garden, until Maggie rushes tearfully away.

Chapter 7, *pp. 524–38*

Maggie encounters Philip Wakem again. Philip feels that Maggie may
have changed, and senses a developing relationship between Maggie and
Stephen.

Chapter 8, *pp. 539–46*

Philip shows his father some sketches he has done, including the two of
Maggie. Philip goes on to reveal his love for Maggie. Although initially
angered, Mr Wakem agrees to the match and adds that he will sell the mill
to Guest and Co.

Chapter 9, *pp. 547–57*

A bazaar is held in the medieval hall of St Ogg's. Philip and Stephen vie
for Maggie's attentions, and she feels sympathy for the widowed Dr
Kenn. Maggie confides in Lucy that she will seek another teaching post
and not marry Philip.

Chapter 10, *pp. 558–64*

At a dance in the Guest household Stephen and Maggie go into the
conservatory. Stephen kisses Maggie's arm; she feels angry and ashamed
about her betrayal of Lucy. Philip calls the following day and she assures
him it is only her feelings for her brother which keeps them apart.

Chapter 11, *pp. 565–72*

Maggie goes to see her aunt, Mrs Moss. Stephen appears unexpectedly,
and asks her to marry him. She admits that she loves him.

Chapter 12, *pp. 573–80*

A family party at the Pullets' house celebrates the Tullivers' return to the old mill. Lucy reveals to Tom the part that Philip Wakem played in regaining the property, but Tom insists that Maggie can never marry Philip.

Chapter 13, *pp. 581–95*

Maggie returns to St Ogg's and continues to see Stephen Guest. Lucy proposes a plan whereby she and her father will travel to a village on the river where they will be met by Maggie and Philip who will row there. Philip is so upset by the growing warmth between Maggie and Stephen that he cannot go. Stephen arrives and persuades Maggie to let him row her downstream. She acts automatically as in a dream, and the boat drifts past the appointed place before Maggie realizes what is happening. The couple board a passing trading-ship and Maggie falls asleep.

Chapter 14, *pp. 596–607*

On awakening, Maggie feels that she has sinned. She rejects Stephen's impassioned pleas and argues that they cannot build their happiness on the misery of others. She begins the lonely journey back to St Ogg's.

Book VII

Maggie gets back to St Ogg's in late June 1839, and begins work for Dr Kenn in July. The flood occurs in the second week of September. The Conclusion looks forward to 1844 and later years.

Chapter 1, *pp. 611–18*

Tom's happiness at regaining possession of the mill is blighted by his sister's behaviour. Maggie now appears at Dorlcote, but Tom repudiates her for her actions. He will continue to support her financially, but says that she cannot live any longer at the mill. With her mother, Maggie goes to stay with Bob Jakin at St Ogg's.

Chapter 2, *pp. 619–28*

The narrator ruminates upon the notion that St Ogg's might have accepted Stephen and Maggie if they had married and returned to the town after a period of months. This is in marked contrast to the social ostracism and gossip which the heroine now faces from a censorious and conventionally minded community. Maggie herself is more worried about Lucy and Philip. Dr Kenn, a sympathetic and mature listener, advises her to leave the little town. She insists, however, upon the fact that she must stay in her native place.

Chapter 3, *pp. 629–35*

Mrs Glegg proves a surprising ally in the crisis, and acts out of loyalty to the family. She is unable, however, to persuade Tom to take Maggie back at the mill. Philip writes a letter to Maggie expressing his sympathy and love for her.

Chapter 4, *pp. 636–43*

Dr Kenn is deeply alarmed by the social rejection facing Maggie in St Ogg's, and asks her to look after his children. This move inspires rumours that she plans to marry him. Lucy, about to set off for a recuperative holiday, is reconciled with Maggie.

Chapter 5, *pp. 644–55*

In the autumnal storms of early September, Maggie feels very lonely. She has given up going to Dr Kenn's because of malicious gossip. A letter from Stephen asks her again to marry him. Praying for strength to resist, Maggie becomes aware of water entering the room. She and Bob each take a boat, and Maggie is carried away by the strong current. She finally reaches the mill, and rescues her brother from the floods. Tom accepts that she was innocent, and they are reconciled. They go on to rescue Lucy, but their boat is sunk by a huge piece of machinery and they die in one another's arms.

Conclusion, *pp. 656–7*

Five years have elapsed. Tom and Maggie have been buried together in a grave which is frequently visited by Stephen Guest and by the lonely Philip Wakem. Some years later Stephen and Lucy are to be married.

8. Analysis

The Narrative Voice

Close analysis of the text might fruitfully begin with a consideration of the author's 'voice' in the narrative, and with the relationship which we as readers enjoy with that voice. The question of our relationship with the material of the story and with the implied author is crucial in our understanding of the story, and can only be fully explored by a close analysis of representative passages of prose. As we read this long book we need to be constantly alert to the effects George Eliot is seeking, to the different purposes of the prose at different moments, and to the stylistic techniques utilized to gain these effects. *The Mill on the Floss*, in the richness and density of its prose, the variety and divergence of its aims, needs to be attended to with some of the close scrutiny that we would normally reserve for the reading of poetry. The more closely the reader is familiar with the text the more fully will George Eliot's purpose and achievement be made clear.

The Mill on the Floss marks a distinct stage in the development of the English novel. In this text, concern for the moral awareness of the characters is emphasized and foregrounded over external events. While we remember the central actions – Maggie's hair-cropping, Tulliver's fight, the meetings at the Red Deeps, the boat journey, the bazaar, the flood, for instance – we are also aware that these events depend upon other, inner events which precede or follow on from them. These inner events are the stuff of George Eliot's fiction, in its concern for moral choice and action, and they are characteristically expressed through free indirect speech. The widespread usage of free indirect speech in the novel enables the author (or implied speaker) to range widely from humorous or satiric reflections to an investigation of decisive moments of moral choice, such as Maggie's return to St Ogg's from Mudport. The investigation of these complex points of crisis remains firmly in the hands of the narrator, and it is this narrator who establishes the morality and perspective of the story that is being told. This being said, we might usefully go on to distinguish two narrators in the text: one an 'impersonal' narrator/historian, and the second an authorial 'second self' who uses 'I' and 'me' in speaking to us as readers, and enunciating truths about life. There is of course no hard and fast division between the two voices we may hear in the narrative thread, but the social historian is more evident for instance in the intro-

ductory analysis of the Dodsons, and the 'second self' in such inter-
jections as 'Do not think too hardly of Philip' (p. 430). In order to give
us a very full and rich sense of living among these characters as moral
beings George Eliot employs report, description, commentary, dialogue
and inner monologue. While the privileged access to thought of free
indirect speech is most marked in the presentation of Maggie, where it is
used to make us feel close to the heroine, it is also employed quite as
successfully with lesser figures. Here, for instance, is Mrs Glegg inspecting
Mrs Tulliver's millinery:

> This was part of Bessy's weakness that stirred Mrs Glegg's sisterly compassion:
> Bessy went far too well drest, considering; and she was too proud to dress her child
> in the good clothing her sister Glegg gave her from the primeval strata of her
> wardrobe; it was a sin and a shame to buy anything to dress that child, if it wasn't
> a pair of shoes.   (p. 115)

Phrases like 'considering' and 'a sin and a shame' are signs of the free
indirect speech – direct access to the thought processes of Mrs Glegg –
which predominates after the authorial irony of the opening statement.
This kind of imitation speech is equally effective in giving us some sense
of Tom's feelings and ambitions while under the hard tutelage of Mr
Stelling:

> He was not going to be a snuffy schoolmaster   he; but a substantial man, like
> his father, who used to go hunting when he was younger, and rode a capital black
> mare – as pretty a bit of horse-flesh as ever you saw: Tom had heard what her points
> were a hundred times.   (p. 201)

Here Tom identifies closely with his father as a way of compensating for
his lack of classical aptitude, and the effects of the language are at the
same time slightly satirical of Tom's thoughts and aims. Within the two
passages George Eliot successfully inhabits the very different mental
worlds of a fussy, worldly matron and a boisterous schoolboy. Novels are
comprised of nothing but language, and it is well worth noting the great
range of such effects which George Eliot has at her command in peopling
the novel.

While Tom and Mrs Glegg are subtly ironized, where the author feels
a deeper sympathy with the character the language loses this ironic level.
We may see this when Maggie goes home after her interview with Philip:

> I said that Maggie went home that evening ... with a mental conflict already
> begun. You have seen clearly enough in her interview with Philip, what that conflict
> was. Here suddenly was an opening in the rocky wall which shut in the narrow
> Valley of Humiliation, where all her prospect was the remote unfathomed sky; and

some of the memory-haunting earthly delights were no longer out of her reach. She might have books, converse, affection – she might hear tidings of the world from which her mind had not yet lost its sense of exile; and it would be a kindness to Philip too, who was pitiable – clearly not happy;   (p. 424)

In a passage like this (and there are many others in the novel) authorial comment and Maggie's own reflections are subtly intermingled. Such terms as 'might have' and 'might hear' show us that it is Maggie reflecting, yet at the same time 'remote unfathomed sky' sounds distinctly authorial. The skilled intermingling here may be compared with the passage on Mrs Glegg, where the phrase 'primeval strata of her wardrobe' stands out from the rest of the passage, referring as it does to the Victorian intellectual interest in geology which Mrs Glegg very evidently would not have shared with George Eliot herself. The character here, and to a lesser extent Maggie, lives in a more restricted world than the author, and this limitation is registered through language everywhere in the text. The characters do not 'live' somewhere outside that text, they are essentially creations of language and linguistic effects. The act of creating character through such passages is the act of communication as between author and reader. Where the character is relatively minor, the author gives herself a wider satiric licence, as when Bob Jakin picks up the knife he had thrown back to Tom:

> The knife would do no good on the ground there ... And there were two blades – and they had just been sharpened. What is life without a pocket-knife to him who has once tasted a higher existence? No: to throw the handle after the hatchet is a comprehensible act of desperation, but to throw one's pocket-knife after an implacable friend is clearly in every sense a hyperbole ...   (p. 106)

The thought processes of Bob are gently mocked here, his idea of a 'higher existence' held up to a mildly superior ridicule which nevertheless does not dissolve our sympathy with his gentle nature. The intervention of the implied author is most complicated perhaps at the moments of critical choice, as when Maggie is carried along in the boat with Stephen:

> There were moments in which a cruel selfishness seemed to be getting possession of her: why should not Lucy – why should not Philip suffer? *She* had had to suffer through many years of her life, and who had renounced anything for her? And when something like that fullness of existence – love, wealth, ease, refinement – all that her nature craved was brought within her reach, why was she to forego [sic] it, that another might have it – another, who perhaps needed it less?   (p. 582)

The question of 'what her nature craved' may relate more evidently to the author's awareness than the character's, and perhaps it applies to a calmer frame of mind than any that Maggie could have commanded at that time. But the passage brings vividly before us the sense of her anxious cogitation in all its vacillating movement. *The Mill on the Floss* is both a novel of narration, a story told to us by a reliable narrator, and also a novel of self-narration in which characters can be entrusted with parts of their own story and sense of values.

The narrative line of *The Mill on the Floss* depends upon a number of conflicts and disturbances: Tulliver's disputes with Pivart and Wakem, the tensions between the Dodsons and the Tullivers, Tom's dislike of Philip, Maggie's relationship with Tom, and so on. The conventions of the nineteenth-century novel demanded that all of these elements of conflict must ultimately be settled or closed. What is often termed as 'closure' indicates that some kind of order must be re-established in the world of the story, as in George Eliot's Conclusion here, where we are assured that 'Nature repairs her ravages' (p. 656). A form of fiction is required, then, in which order is restored through crisis and resolution. It is only with hindsight that we, as readers, are able to comprehend the total pattern – to see, for example, how Mr Tulliver's tragic fall may foreshadow that of his daughter. This pattern of meaning is achieved through the language, the description, analysis and dialogue whose subtleties we have already noted. The layers of such writing are very complex, as may be seen when Mr Tulliver rides to his sister, Mrs Moss:

Mr Tulliver gave his horse a little stroke on the flank, then checked it and said angrily, 'Stand still with you!' much to the astonishment of that innocent animal.

'And the more there is of 'em, the more they must love one another,' Mrs Moss went on, looking at her children with a didactic purpose. But she turned towards her brother again to say, 'Not but what I hope your boy 'ull allays be good to his sister, though there's but two of 'em, like you and me, brother.'

That arrow went straight to Mr Tulliver's heart. He had not a rapid imagination, but the thought of Maggie was very near to him, and he was not long in seeing his relation to his own sister side by side with Tom's relation to Maggie. Would the little wench ever be poorly off, and Tom rather hard upon her?

'Ay, ay, Gritty,' said the miller, with a new softness in his tone. 'But I've allays done what I could for you,' he added, as if vindicating himself from a reproach.

(pp. 140–41)

Catherine Belsey interestingly shows, in *Critical Practice*, how in such a passage of 'classic realism' the reader is aware, but may not be fully conscious of, a clear division between the conversation which is carried on and reported and the authorial interpretation of that conversation. What we are encountering is the interpretation on our behalf by a privileged narrator who gives the entire story a coherent gloss. Throughout a long work like *The Mill on the Floss* we must attune ourselves to this privileged voice and the ways it is operating on us as readers. In this episode Mr Tulliver is aware of a wider relevance than Mrs Moss, because of her limited intelligence, can command; yet he is a good deal less aware than we, as readers, because of the hidden mediation or intervention of the narrator. It is this intervening voice which assures us that 'he was not long in seeing his relation to his own sister side by side with Tom's relation to Maggie'. This does not imply the narrator's continual interference. On the contrary, when Mr Tulliver irritably checks his horse, we are left to tease out the meaning for ourselves. The reader and the author, in this kind of realistic narrative, create the work between them. The final meaning of the work (if there is such a thing) is a product of the collaboration between ourselves and the author, and that type of collaboration depends much upon the realistic creation of character. In other words, there is a secret 'contract' between the author and ourselves which operates to create a world we may accept as real.

Realism

The question of 'realism' is a vexed one in literary criticism, but George Eliot clearly marks herself out as a realist first and foremost. In 'Amos Barton', one of her *Scenes of Clerical Life*, she challenged those who wanted to read of an ideal world, and mocked the weak-headedness of a public who demanded romantic and escapist fictions. Amos Barton, she confesses, is 'unmistakably commonplace'; but it is on ordinary lives that literature should concentrate its efforts: 'is there not a pathos in their very insignificance – in our comparison of their dim and narrow existence with the glorious possibilities of that human nature which they share?' She was reacting against the fashionable literature of the day, and her trenchant article of 1856 on 'Silly Novels by Lady Novelists' condemned the plethora of 'remarkable novels, full of striking situations, thrilling incidents, and eloquent writing' which were then flooding the fiction market through the circulating libraries. Against this trend, George Eliot told the public, 'I only try to exhibit some things as they have been seen.' This does not mean that she ever remains content in her novels with naturalistic or journalistic observation of the world. On the contrary, she is most often concerned to explore the extraordinary within the ordinary and everyday, insisting always on the need to avoid exaggeration, convention and literary artifice: 'Falsehood is so easy, truth so difficult.'

It is this principle that governs George Eliot's treatment of provincial life, and we might fruitfully ponder her defence of the choice of subject matter in Book I V, Chapter 3. She anticipates here the 'oppressive feeling' the enlightened reader may experience in contemplating life by the Floss:

It is a sordid life, you say, this of the Tullivers and Dodsons – irradiated by no sublime principles, no romantic visions, no active, self-renouncing faith ... Here, one has conventional worldly notions and habits without instruction and without polish.   (p. 362)

But this is the very context in which Maggie must live and develop, her evolving career explained as a part of 'the onward tendency of human things' to rise 'above the mental level of the generation before them, to which they have been nevertheless tied by the strongest fibres of their hearts' (p. 363). Contemplation of such provincial matters, such 'unfashionable families', is not liked in polite society, which is in fact founded in the exploitation of others:

This wide national life is based entirely on emphasis – the emphasis of want, which urges it into all the activities necessary for the maintenance of good society and light irony.   (p. 385)

The examination of this 'national life' is governed, in George Eliot's fiction, by her belief in universal laws. Man is felt to be progressing, yet, as Maggie's career so vividly exemplifies, man is a creature of emotion and irrationality. It may be, indeed, that in *The Mill on the Floss* her fidelity to empirical realism, exhibiting things 'as they have been or are', clashes with her idealism, which determines Maggie's ultimate and initially controversial fate. 'Realism', that is to say, is a slippery term which presupposes some kind of objective viewpoint. It may be argued that the style of the novel is more successful in the early Books in creating through adult language and judgement, and ironic deflation, detachment from the limitations of Maggie's mind and personality. The careful creation of character and environment in the novel is eminently realistic, and yet quietly symbolic, as here in the presentation of Mr and Mrs Glegg:

Mrs Glegg had both a front and a back parlour in her excellent house at St Ogg's, so that she had two points of view from which she could observe the weaknesses of her fellow-beings and reinforce her thankfulness for her own exceptional strength of mind. From her front windows she could look down the Tofton Road leading out of St Ogg's and note the growing tendency to 'gadding about' in the wives of men not retired from business, together with a practice of wearing woven cotton stockings, which opened a dreary prospect for the coming generation; and from her back windows she could look down the pleasant garden and orchard which stretched to the river, and observe the folly of Mr Glegg in spending his time among 'them flowers and vegetables.'   (pp. 185–6)

The prime function in this passage is to define Mrs Glegg, and its effects are subtle and calculated. The note of irony is reached in Mrs Glegg's 'exceptional strength of mind', since this is Mrs Glegg's valuation, not ours, and this note builds up into her observation of 'the weaknesses of her fellow-beings'. The liking for 'gadding about' and woven stockings is framed within the windows of Mrs Glegg's observation point, social mobility set against the Dodson values of property and stability. To the rear the garden and orchard afford Mrs Glegg ample opportunity for further criticism, this time addressed to her husband's proclivities for horticulture. The well-furnished house and the garden and orchard act as a metaphor for the Gleggs' comfortable existence; the passage goes beyond realistic description into social and moral judgements subtly conveyed in the text. A highly educated syntax and diction is here combined cunningly with ignorant ideas and colloquial diction to create a finely balanced tone of comic seriousness. The 'realism' here, as in other passages, is an effect of language, a language embedded in social and personal memory and expressive of a whole way of life. Such creative language, George Eliot held, could never be scientific. Indeed, a language with 'no uncertainty, no whims of idiom, no hoary archaisms' would never express life itself, 'which is a great deal more then science' (*Essays*. pp. 287–8).

Character in the Novel

1. The Creation of Character

George Eliot held that, as she once put it, 'Art is the nearest thing to life.' Her markedly realistic aims are directly reflected in her approach to character. In *The Mill on the Floss*, as elsewhere in her work, she is primarily concerned with ordinary life. Her role as omniscient narrator enables her to encompass the full range of character around the Floss without strain. Her characterization in the novel, though limited in social range, does allow for many subtle differentiations. There are, for instance, characters who act functionally. These people help to effect movement of the plot, or to enunciate an ethical dilemma. Functional characters of the first type might include Mr and Mrs Stelling, Mr Wakem or even Bob Jakin, while Dr Kenn evidently acts as a normative moral touchstone in the later part of the book. On a different scale, but perhaps also best approached functionally, are the Dodsons. The sisters are notably referred to in the plural, and their treatment reflects the sociological strength of George Eliot's interests. They are neatly distinguished from one another through various character traits, but remain obstinately grouped together in the reader's mind. They represent a significant strand of Victorian society, and function as emblems of that strand within the 'world' of the novel. George Eliot displays her genius characteristically in her realization of the detail of dress and talk of these characters, with their particular ways of bleaching linen, making cowslip wine, taking medicine, making wills and dying. Although the way of life of these provincial women is profoundly accumulative and 'having', its narrowness and pagan lack of spirituality are carefully balanced in the narrator's critical estimate by the Dodson code of honesty and integrity. While each of the sisters is capable of rising wonderfully to individual life, as in Mrs Glegg's scene with Bob Jakin, their voice in the life of the novel is fundamentally a communal one.

At a second level we may identify a range of characters who are more fully evolved and delineated, though none of them possesses the range and depth of Maggie as a protagonist. Their function is to mediate between the background, choric figures and the heroine. Clearly the most important of these middling figures would be the Tulliver family. Tom and Maggie's parents are delineated with unfeigned creative delight and plenitude by George Eliot, yet they are still utilized in a strictly functional way as agents of Maggie's formation. Mrs Tulliver, though rather passive and pathetic in herself, affects the plot radically by her clandestine meeting with Wakem. George Eliot captures with peculiar accuracy the turns of speech of such a character, representing as she does a debilitated strain of the Dodson line. In terms of E. M. Forster's distinction between 'flat' and 'round' characters, Mrs Tulliver remains 'flat', readily identifiable and unchanging. So, in a sense, does Mr Tulliver. But George Eliot's aims and effects here are recognizably more ambitious. Tulliver is a powerfully drawn character who draws down destruction upon his own head. He is proud, wilful and puzzled by the changes affecting St Ogg's. He is a loving father, protective brother and humane master. Despite these sterling qualities he goes to the wall, defeated partly by circumstance, but primarily through his own intransigent failure to adapt. In the portrait of Mr Tulliver, partly drawn from her own father, George Eliot notably allows the character its own inner life and logic. Yet in thinking back over the full reach of the novel we surely recognize Tulliver as fixed and static. Against his tragic *fixity*, we can measure Maggie's equally tragic development. All novels give us a pattern of human relationships, and our awareness of relations determines, to an extent, our response to character. Mr Tulliver, thus, is perceived by us successively or simultaneously as husband, brother, brother-in-law, father, employer, litigant and so on.

Our sense of Mr Tulliver the man is highly dependent upon the delineation of these relationships within which he functions, though it is a measure of his stature that he is not contained within them.

2. George Eliot and Maggie

It may be argued that the psychological elements of the novel to some extent subvert or undermine the surface realism. F. R. Leavis, in *The Great Tradition*, argued that the author lacks full understanding of Maggie through her own immaturity, and particularly through her own too close identification with the heroine. Leavis urges that 'To understand immaturity would be to "place" it ... by relating it to mature experience. But when George Eliot touches on these given intensities of Maggie's inner life the valuation comes directly and simply from the novelist, precluding the presence of a maturer intelligence than Maggie's own.' It is at these points in the narrative, Leavis holds, 'that we are most likely to make with conscious critical intent the comment that in George Eliot's presentment of Maggie there is an element of self-idealization. The criticism sharpens itself when we say that with the self-idealization there goes an element of self-pity.' If valid, this is a telling and damaging critique. The beginnings of a rebuttal might usefully be made by looking at one of these crisis points in the narrative, when George Eliot's involvement might well be thought to overbalance the narrator's impartial sympathy. An instance would be the episode of Bob Jakin's gift of the books in Book IV, and particularly the passage of commentary when Maggie first reads Thomas à Kempis's renunciatory words (pp. 383–4). The diction here, in the analysis of Maggie's emotions, quietly suggests a residue of egotism in the heroine even at this point of spiritual renewal. The narrator, for instance, notes how 'renunciation seemed to her the entrance into that *satisfaction* which she had so long been craving in vain' [my italics] (p 384). It is communicated to the reader that Maggie is immature, since she had not perceived 'the inmost truth of the old monk's outpourings', but instead is seen as 'panting for happiness' and 'in ecstasy because she had found the key' (ibid.) to life. There is fleeting irony also in the dwindling of Maggie's religious 'ardour' into this adolescent 'panting'. The narrator in this crucial scene broadens her analysis to encompass the contrast between the aims and ambitions of 'good society' with a 'wide and arduous national life' founded upon 'the emphasis of want' (p. 385). The result is that when we return to Maggie we are prepared to accept her as an example of a social group who feel higher aspirations than circumstance allows. George Eliot here, as so often in the novel, unites character creation with function. To say this is not to deny that in the portrait of Maggie she is reaching down into some of her deepest childhood experiences. Certainly the novel contains a portrait of someone dependent on 'the need of being loved', and upon the potency of memory. The two factors combine in her as they did in her creator, as she acknowledges when Philip alleges that she can never accord him the love she feels for Tom:

> 'Perhaps not,' said Maggie, simply, 'but then, you know, the first thing I ever remember in my life is standing with Tom by the side of the Floss while he held my hand – everything before that is dark to me.'   (pp. 402–3)

Full of 'eager, passionate longings for all that was beautiful and glad', Maggie is also 'thirsty for all knowledge', and these aspirations militate against her wholehearted acceptance of the life and culture of St Ogg's. What George Eliot attempts here is an analysis of a girl living and growing in the patriarchal society of mid-Victorian England. Accorded a frivolous education, Maggie attempts to resolve some of her disappointments through her cult of self-renunciation, but this is coolly shown by the narrator to be wilful suppression of vital sources of her energy and identity.

Throughout the novel Maggie is prey to her own 'hungry nature': she desires love, affection and union. To satisfy this desire she seeks the approval of a number of love-objects – her father, Tom, Philip, Stephen Guest – and at the same time tries to deny herself through asceticism and the call of duty. Her desires are frequently frustrated by the action, and are finally only satisfied by the flood. Although that scene, which will be examined in detail later, records a final loving embrace between brother and sister, the earlier childhood scenes do not endorse that vision of blissful union. In George Eliot's 'Brother and Sister' sonnets (1869), the brother appears to be protective, demanding and rigid. When he takes his sister fishing he scolds her for neglecting the line but praises her for hooking a perch. The girl by contrast is worshipful, sensitive, eager for praise, and together they learn:

> *the meanings that give words a soul,*
> *The fear, the love, the principal passionate store,*
> *Whose shaping impulses make mankind whole.*

The sister says of the brother:

> *His years with others must the sweeter be*
> *For those brief days he spent in loving me.*

Tom Tulliver is not Isaac Evans, but we may detect in the early sections of the novel something of Mary Ann's affection for her brother, and in Tom's rejection of Maggie after the flight with Stephen Guest there is a note reminiscent of Isaac's respectable outrage at Mary Ann's cohabiting with Lewes. Brother and sister show the crucial significance of inheritance: Mr Tulliver justly remarks that Tom is 'a bit slowish' (p. 59), while Maggie is 'twice as cute. Too cute for a woman, I'm afraid' (pp. 59–60). Maggie's first speech, as she enters dishevelled from the river, aligns her against the orderliness and propriety of the Dodsons. She is emotionally drawn to Mrs Moss, to whom Mr Tulliver shows mercy in the hope that Tom will protect Maggie similarly. The Dodsons, and Tom, are characterized by 'a proud, honest egoism, which had a hearty dislike to whatever made against its own credit or interest' (p. 365). 'I have found *my* comfort in doing my duty' (p. 613), Tom informs his sister. In the light of his hardness, some critics have found Maggie's love for Tom incomprehensible. She herself says, 'You have been reproaching other people all your life – you have always been sure you yourself are right.' Yet Tom of course has many good impulses also, as when asked to look after the Stellings' baby daughter, or in his determination to pay off the creditors without drawing on Mr Moss's promissory note. George Eliot claimed that she had portrayed Tom 'with as much love and pity as Maggie'. It is his hard-faced independence which perhaps sacrifices some of the reader's sympathy, and intensifies the contrast with Maggie, with her craving for sympathy and affection. The narrator sees her eyes 'full of unsatisfied intelligence and unsatisfied, beseeching affection'. To the extent that these qualities are inherited from the narrator, it can be argued, the novel may be flawed. We may wish to discriminate, however, between the Maggie whose confusions and immaturity are comprehended and placed by this narrator and a Maggie whose 'destiny' reveals some loss of authorial control and perspective. A passage from Tom's schooling illuminates this:

In the afternoon, the boys were at their books in the study, preparing the morrow's lessons, that they might have a holiday in the evening in honour of Maggie's arrival. Tom was hanging over his Latin grammar, moving his lips inaudibly like a strict but impatient Catholic repeating his tale of paternosters, and Philip, at the other end of the room, was busy with two volumes, with a look of contented diligence that excited Maggie's curiosity: he did not look at all as if he were learning a lesson. She sat on a low stool at nearly a right angle with the two boys, watching first one and then the other, and Philip looking off his book once towards the fireplace, caught the pair of questioning dark eyes fixed upon him. He thought this sister of Tulliver's seemed a nice little thing, quite unlike her brother: he wished *he* had a little sister. What was it, he wondered, that made Maggie's dark eyes remind him of the stories about princesses being turned into animals? ... I think it was, that her eyes were full of unsatisfied intelligence and unsatisfied, beseeching affection. (pp. 252–3)

In this finely imagined scene a most significant point is the centrality of Maggie: she is physically dominant, as she is thematically dominant throughout the novel. Philip Wakem's unspoken desire for a sister neatly dramatizes her own relations with Tom and with Philip himself, as opposing types of male. Philip's identification of her with a princess changed into an animal perhaps denotes a denial of her true inner nature, while the emotionally charged language of the final sentence here marks a slip into the subjective mode by the objective narrator. The great expressive eyes, which dominate so many Victorian paintings, for instance, form here a symbol for all that is unfulfilled in the heroine, but, more damagingly perhaps, in her creator also.

Despite the central placement of Maggie, she does not function as the kind of central intelligence we meet in Henry James. On the contrary, in the presentation of all the strands of *The Mill on the Floss*, George Eliot appears to adopt a multiple perspective. Parts of the book, for instance, are dominated by Mr Tulliver, and Tom's schooling deliberately places Maggie at the margins of the action for a time. The unity of experience, therefore, is that of the author, not of the character. Within Maggie herself there is no fixed centre, since she vacillates between the tendency to self-sacrifice and the desire for self-indulgence and fulfilment. As a result she finds it hard to strike a balance with the other characters, or indeed with herself.

3. *Renunciation and Illusion*

In the treatment of self-sacrifice, George Eliot takes steps towards incorporating the notion of the 'higher religion' of human sympathy into her fiction. The moment of liberation for Maggie comes when she reads, in *The Imitation of Christ*, 'a secret of life that would enable her to renounce all other secrets' (p. 383). In this volume, the narrator explains, 'was insight, and strength, and conquest, to be won by means entirely within her own soul, where a supreme teacher was waiting to be heard' (pp. 383–4). George Eliot is careful to alert the reader to the point that Maggie has not been inculcated into some kind of dogmatic Christianity: 'It flashed through her like the suddenly apprehended solution of a problem, that all the miseries of her young life had come from fixing her heart on her own pleasure' (p. 384). Maggie, that is to say, has not become a Catholic, since she knows 'nothing of doctrines and systems' (ibid.). The implication and meaning of the passage from the *Imitation* emphasizes renunciation of the self. We might be able to discern here the guarded tone of an agnostic writer working within a conventionally Christian society, but George Eliot moves beyond this in praising 'resignation for ourselves and active love for what is not ourselves' (p. 386). She is endorsing a kind of 'enthusiasm' and emotional warmth which does not derive from personal happiness. Yet paradoxically the narrator acknowledges that Maggie was 'panting for happiness, and was in ecstasy because she had found the key to it' (p. 384) – the renunciation of her personal wishes. Maggie's experiences are sympathetically drawn here as part of an adolescent crisis of personality, and it is necessarily only one stage of her complex development. The keynote of the novel, it may be, is not so much the heroine's relations with society as the relationship with herself. While *The Mill on the Floss* deals with the process of growing to maturity, the novel does not see maturity as some kind of end-point to be reached. The crisis with the wooden doll may stand as an emblem of a recurrent pattern in Maggie's life, with its sense of disaster, its giving over of the heroine to the emotion of the moment, and then a feeling of deliverance and exaltation:

Since then, she had driven no more nails in, but had soothed herself by alternately grinding and beating the wooden head against the rough brick of the great chimneys that made two square pillars supporting the roof. That was what she did this morning on reaching the attic, sobbing all the while with a passion that expelled every other form of consciousness – even the memory of the grievance that had caused it. As at last the sobs were getting quieter and the grinding less fierce, a sudden beam of sunshine, falling through the wire lattice across the worm-eaten shelves, made her throw away the Fetish and run to the window.   (p. 79)

The structure of the novel in one sense consists of a series of objective situations which produce an identical subjective response in Maggie. As the novel moves onwards, however, the pattern seems to change, and the possibility of joy arising out of suffering diminishes. When Mr Tulliver is taken ill the narrator writes:

Poor child! It was very early for her to know one of those supreme moments in life when all we have hoped or delighted in, all we can dread or endure, falls away from our regard as insignificant, – is lost, like a trivial memory, in that simple, primitive love which knits us to the beings who have been nearest to us, in their times of helplessness or of anguish.   (p. 278)

The sense of desolation within encroaches more as the plot moves forward. Maggie is in the grip of fact, her sense of self blighted by the outer world. Only in the ending, where she and Tom are transformed beyond the reach of time, can she escape from this process. St Ogg's and Tom fail Maggie equally, and the two failures coincide when they ostracize her for her escapade with Stephen Guest. Maggie's lack of knowledge of this hard real world is characterized as conflict between imagination and fact: 'everybody in the world seemed so hard and unkind to Maggie: there was no indulgence, no fondness, such as she imagined when she fashioned the world afresh in her own thoughts' (p. 319). Maggie's imaginary world, we might say, has no referent, and she prefers a bookishly imagined world to the reality of St Ogg's. The collision between such illusion and the real is clearly demonstrated to her when she runs off to the gypsies. Fiction has the power, therefore, to make her unhappy, as she recognizes when she refuses Philip's gift of Scott's *The Pirate,* because it will make her 'want too much' (p. 402). Desire for Maggie is without limit, and needs to be checked by responsibility. Her love for Stephen Guest seems to her divorced from the context of her past and family ties, so that only the desires related to memory are endorsed fully by the novel. Sexual desire seems to be felt as dangerous and disturbing. Maggie's relationship with Tom is of course prior to sexual awakening, and it is to this desire that she ultimately returns. The dominant sense Maggie has is one of exile from her own idealized past. George Eliot's fascination with moral choice and indecision, however, means that Maggie cannot fully choose between different sides of her own nature, between, say, Tom and Philip, or Tom and Stephen, just as she first batters her doll fetish against the wall and then gives it a make-believe poultice. This kind of oscillation is at the heart of her nature, and it operates clearly in her simultaneously desired renunciation of pleasure and clandestine meetings in the Red Deeps, and most momentously in her relationship with Stephen Guest. The patterning of the novel is founded in this pendulum movement between passion and its denial, fulfilment and renunciation. Maggie's conversations in the Red Deeps represent an alternative to the local community and culture, and yet they clash with her earliest ties and duties. In describing the brother and sister idyllically fishing at the Round Pool, the narrator notes how the flowers, birds, sky and fields 'are the mother-tongue of our imagination, the language that is laden with all the subtle inextricable associations the fleeting hours of our childhood left behind them' (p. 94). It is this secret 'language' to which Maggie most intimately responds and adheres: 'If the past is not to bind us, where can duty lie?' (pp. 601–2), she demands of Stephen Guest after being 'borne along by the tide'. Yet the Wordsworthian myth of childhood she implicitly appeals to here does not seem to tally with the facts of her relationship with Tom: the Round Pool is virtually the only time the pair experience unblemished happiness together.

Attitudes to place in *The Mill on the Floss* are characteristically ambiguous: place seems both sacred and idyllic, and narrow and confining. This ambivalence is registered in the prose: at the opening of the story the tone is intimate and pastoral, as the narrator tells us of the stream, the trees and branches, and then moves on to the little girl watching the mill-wheel. From this dreamlike opening we turn in the second chapter to the realities of the Tullivers and the problems of Tom's education. The differences in tone between the two chapters (which need careful re-reading) mark the differences in approach between the note of dreamy intimacy with the reader and the shrewd external commentator who is in full control. It is this stylistic ambivalence which feeds in to the creation of the character of Maggie herself. The ideal childhood seems to come to an end at the conclusion of Book II:

> They had gone forth together into their new life of sorrow, and they would never more see the sunshine undimmed by remembered cares. They had entered the thorny wilderness, and the golden gates of their childhood had for ever closed behind them.   (p. 270)

This elegiac note is often hard to reconcile with Maggie's real experiences of growing up at the mill. Raymond Williams has noticed this feature of George Eliot's fiction, what he calls the break 'between the narrative idea of the novelist and the overwhelming emphasis on emotion'. This break may be a tension between an ideal of communal life and a commitment to personal evolution and moral development. To an extent the narrator seems herself unaware of the contradictions in the handling of childhood, and those contradictions may be located within the author herself. However, these contradictions are expressed in narrative form, and it is necessary for the reader to be aware of the psychological conflicts and patterns which underlie (and may even at times undermine) Maggie's experience of life. Her constant desire is for love and understanding, and the long childhood relationship with her brother may fruitfully be read in the light of this need.

4. Brother and Sister

After confessing to Tom about the death of his rabbits, and her brother's brusque response, the heroine feels the 'need of being loved, the strongest need in poor Maggie's nature' (p. 89), and Tom reconciles himself with her through the gift of cake. Food also features in the incident of the jam puffs, and the narrator comments here, 'I fear she cared less that Tom should enjoy the utmost possible amount of puff than that he should be pleased with her for giving him the best bit' (p. 99). The greed here, as later in the novel, is for love, and it is in such trivial episodes that the author subtly creates our sense of Maggie's personality. In the visit to the Round Pool, brother and sister experience their only united happiness, and it may be that the description of the pond, in its circularity and depth, represents a return to a womb-like existence now denied to the growing children:

that wonderful pool, which the floods had made a long while ago: no one knew how deep it was; and it was mysterious too that it should be almost a perfect round, framed in with willows and tall reeds, so that the water was only to be seen when you got close to the brink.   (p. 92)

With hindsight the reader classifies the pond with other places of retreat such as the attic, where Maggie 'expelled every other form of consciousness' (p. 79), and the 'great spaces of the mill' which make her feel it is 'a little world apart from her outside everyday life' (p. 80). These moments of retreat are marks of unconformity with the outer world, and especially with the world-view of the Dodsons, as relayed to Maggie by Mrs Tulliver. Maggie's deviations from the Dodsons' 'way' cause Mrs Tulliver great anguish, and she is constantly peevish and critical of her wilful child. Mrs Tulliver, 'fair, plump, and dull-witted', has through her disappointments turned a little sour in a way which 'may disagree with young stomachs seriously' (p. 62). This maternal lowering of Maggie's self-esteem is compounded by the problems of her gender. Even the practical Mr Tulliver feels that 'an over 'cute woman's no better nor a long-tailed sheep' (p. 60). Maggie is the very opposite of all that the Dodsons value in the female of the species, and this constant denial of her own value helps to focus her feelings upon Tom so that she senses 'it would make a very nice heaven to sit by the pool in that way, and never be scolded' (p. 93). In an attempt to avoid such scolding and become acceptably feminine like her cousin Lucy, Maggie cuts off her unruly hair with Tom as accomplice. Since throughout literature and art the hair has been a primary symbol of female attraction and difference, the implications of Maggie's action are clear. She is seeking to deny her own inner nature in order to conform with imposed outer standards of appearance and behaviour. Such a seeking is always doomed in the text to bafflement and disappointment, and it is under the pressures wrought by frustration that Maggie will later turn to the crippled Philip:

Maggie moreover had rather a tenderness for deformed things; she preferred the wry-necked lambs, because it seemed to her that the lambs which were quite strong and well made wouldn't mind so much about being petted, and she was especially fond of petting objects that would think it very delightful to be petted by her. She loved Tom very dearly, but she often wished that he *cared* more about her loving him.   (p. 252)

Maggie is thus beginning to seek a substitute for her unresponsive brother under her experience of constant family criticism, but the relationship with Philip is interrupted by Mr Tulliver's downfall. Later, however, Philip becomes both mentor and rescuer, the only character in the novel to recognize the true needs of her inner nature. She, on the other hand, is not fully responsive to his needs, and this drives him to make explicit his love for the miller's daughter. Within the patriarchal society of St Ogg's, Philip must strike the observer as rather lacking in maleness, and this has led Maggie unwittingly to treat him as confidant rather than lover. Upon his declaration, she can only reply rather lamely, 'I think I should never be tired of being with you' (p. 437). His deformity has permitted Maggie to perceive their meetings in the Red Deeps as innocent, even though they clearly run counter to her desire for self-renunciation.

It is Philip Wakem, through his sustained intelligence and sensitivity, who alerts Maggie to a higher cultural and imaginative existence. At the same time his deformity separates him very markedly from the other males in the world of St Ogg's. Philip's artistic gifts are those of the connoisseur rather than the creative spirit, and he finally seems to lack any genuine compensation for the failure of his love for Maggie. His abnormality is disinterestedly described without morbidity, but we observe the faults of temper and jealousy which deformity can give rise to. The triangular relationship with Stephen and Maggie touches upon some painful matters which George Eliot handles firmly. In the upshot Philip is destined by appearance and character to remain a lonely and misunderstood outsider. The intervention of Tom into their rendezvous, though brusque and cruel, is felt as a secret relief by Maggie. The underlying pattern is clear: Maggie offends Tom and is punished, just as she was as a child.

This pattern dominates Maggie's relations with her brother: she forgets the rabbits, knocks over his house of cards, spills his wine, goes out to seek work, ruins the triumphal repayment of the debt through her liaison with Philip. The final drifting away with Stephen Guest at the very point when Tom is able to buy back the mill is simply the culmination of this repeated pattern in the thread of the narrative, a pattern whereby the heroine's alleged sins are punished by the removal of her brother's love. In a very real sense, the flood is the only time that Maggie is permitted to experience a sense of superiority to her implacable sibling, her purposeful rowing here implicitly contrasted with her earlier unconscious drifting along with the tide.

5. *Maggie in Love*

Before this emotional finale, it is necessary that the emotions which Philip has awakened should be fully expressed through his opposite, the vigorous and glamorous figure of Stephen Guest. Stephen seems rather conventionally conceived as an attractive young man of the period. He has not appeared a suitable match for Maggie to all readers (indeed, the Victorian critic Leslie Stephen described him as a 'mere hairdresser's block'). His gaiety and charm are, however, irresistibly linked to economic themes in the novel, and it is stressed that his perfumed appearance is the result 'of the largest oil-mill and the most expensive wharf in St Ogg's' (p. 469). Although he is somewhat woodenly drawn, Guest is different in kind from fops such as young Torry: he is an accomplished singer, well educated and polite in any social circle. Above all, when they meet, he and Maggie are surprised into genuine sexual passion.

In Book VI the effects of this new glamour upon the heroine are explored and dramatized. Maggie, we are shown, takes a keen interest in the musical performances at Lucy's house, and is also highly susceptible to being 'taken care of in that kind graceful manner by some one taller and stronger' (p. 492). This susceptibility issues into the dramatic passivity of the boating sequence, where Maggie feels that 'she was being led down the garden among the roses' by a 'stronger presence' and 'without any act of her own will' (p. 588). At this juncture the narrator adds significantly, 'Memory was excluded' (p. 589). Maggie's potently felt proclivity to be cared for by a stronger male, her longing for love and comfort from her earliest days, her total experience as child and adolescent, culminate in this striking chapter. At last the kind of submerged jealousy of Lucy, which reaches back to the episode when Maggie pushed her into the mud, is brought closer to the surface. Maggie is now transformed into a beautiful young woman, but she finally refuses to use her attraction to hurt her cousin. Yet while on the river she feels enveloped in an 'enchanted haze' (p. 589) which dissipates rapidly when she no longer recognizes her surroundings. None the less, at Stephen's persuasion, she becomes 'paralysed' (p. 591) and yields to his entreaties:

Every influence tended to lull her into acquiescence: that dreamy gliding in the boat, which had lasted for four hours and had brought some weariness and exhaustion – the recoil of her fatigued sensations from the impracticable difficulty of getting out of the boat at this unknown distance from home, and walking for long miles – all helped to bring her into more complete subjection to that strong mysterious charm. (p. 592)

After the young couple board the boat for Mudport, Maggie is upheld by Stephen's support. She begins to hope that there may be 'a life for mortals here below which was not hard and chill – in which affection would no longer be self-sacrifice' (p. 594). However, in her dream of boating with Stephen, the two had passed another boat carrying an uncaring Tom, and we might read this dream-sequence as marking the beginning of the emotional pull back towards early childhood at the end of the novel. Maggie rejects Stephen Guest's pleas, and, the narrator astutely comments, 'almost desired to endure the severity of Tom's reproof, to submit in patient silence to that harsh disapproving judgment against which she had so often rebelled' (p. 612). Maggie's period of atonement within a critical and gossiping St Ogg's culminates in the flood through which she attains Tom's final forgiveness, and the pair are controversially reunited. While the problematic ending requires fuller attention later, sufficient has been said to show that fundamentally the novel is governed by an almost biblical pattern of offence, punishment and reconciliation, and the stages of Maggie's progress are significantly denoted in the titles of each Book. The first two, 'Boy and Girl' and 'School-Time', are redolent with a Wordsworthian sense of childhood and growth, but then 'The Downfall' and 'The Valley of Humiliation', with their glancing references at the underlying scheme of pilgrimage drawn from Bunyan's *The Pilgrim's Progress*, evoke a sense of error, renunciation and homelessness. Maggie's final prayer is, 'O God, where am I? Which is the way home?' (p. 651), and that note resounds throughout the later Books in which she is a 'lonely wanderer' (p. 646).

Society and the Individual

But *The Mill on the Floss* is far more than a psychological narrative. Of all the great nineteenth-century novelists George Eliot is perhaps the one most overtly concerned to explore the interactions between the individual and society. Indeed it is impossible to comprehend Maggie's career, with its vacillating curves of aspiration and renunciation, without the magnificently full examination of the social context. Character is delineated here in relation to economics and culture, because George Eliot has a sociological interest in such defining relations. She once complained, 'How little the real characteristics of the working classes are known to those who are outside them.' Art, she urged, should devote itself to studying 'the natural history of our social classes, especially of the small shop-keepers, artisans, and peasantry' (*Essays*, p. 272). Raymond Williams has suggestively remarked that a dominant concern in the late-Victorian novel is 'what community is, what it has been, what it might be'. The major Victorian novelists, he argues, repeatedly look at the possibility of new social relations and the losses entailed in the 'great social and historical changes which altered not only outward forms – institutions and landscapes – but also inward feelings, experiences, self-definitions'. George Eliot is very much concerned, in *The Mill on the Floss*, with both the 'institutions and landscapes' of the Floss and the experiences and self-definitions of Tom and Maggie.

A purpose of the classic realist text is, clearly, to portray characters and society in the process of development. The people and society of St Ogg's grow and evolve in ways which may be grasped by the mind of the reader. George Eliot is indeed dealing here with the development of a sense of self, a self with its own histories and memories set within a society which is also evolving at a different rate of growth. It is always necessary, in reading fiction, to note the authority of its presentation: Mr Tulliver and Maggie are flawed by their illusions, yet out of them issue movement and change. Against the dynamism of Maggie's inner life, for instance, we may place the paralysis and repetition of the Dodsons. Maggie's project, in which she is repeatedly unsuccessful, is to steer herself clear of obstacles which hurt, stultify or (in the final symbolic collision with the piece of machinery) destroy her. Maggie's renunciation of marriage and child-bearing marks a crucial rejection of what has been termed the 'genealogical imperative' in the English novel – the stress upon generation, continuity and inheritance which marks such works as *Wuthering Heights, Great Expectations* or indeed *Middlemarch*. Maggie is divorced by her creator from her generative role and function, and finally from the continuum of time itself. The chief characteristic of classic realism is that it is expressed through consecutive explanation which allows the author to refer back to whatever has gone before. This action serves to uncover the sense of identity which Maggie embodies splendidly yet tragically in the novel. She possesses a sense of herself as unique and different, and it is this sense which creates the tension between the bonds of community and creative emotional freedom. Maggie's rejection of Stephen must be in some sense a surrender to the social bonds from which her temperament has severed her. Sending Stephen away is an act of self-isolation since she cannot recreate the social milieu of her pre-adolescent period. St Ogg's would ultimately have accepted the marriage, because the society of the town understood and condoned the generative principle which underlay the institution of matrimony. Through the deaths of Maggie and Tom the Tulliver line comes to an end in a manner which challenges the continuity embodied in realist fiction and demanded by its readership; their demise indeed looks forward tentatively to Hardy's doom-laden portrayal in *Jude the Obscure* of the 'coming universal wish not to live'.

The interweaving of public and private values at St Ogg's is exposed with a masterly grasp of the power of tradition and change which had been attained through the author's earlier schooling in the techniques of rationalism and positivism. While demonstrating the 'oppressive narrowness' (p. 363) of the Dodson world, George Eliot also reveals its positive values, the adherence to a coherent world of traditional ties which is now being gradually eroded. That process of erosion is neatly exemplified among the Dodson circle itself. While Mrs Glegg, with her hidden store of lace, fully personifies the 'having' qualities of the family, Mr Deane's rise in the world of commerce demonstrates the opposing forces. Deane, with his admiration for steampower, is an enthusiastic participant in the new commercialism of St Ogg's, an entrepreneur and taker of considered risks. Mrs Glegg still acknowledges, and acts upon, family ties as the mainstay of her life, as we see in her support for the disgraced Maggie. Mr Deane, on the other hand, is at pains to point out that Guest and Co. do not conduct their affairs on what he terms 'sentimental grounds'. The obligations of family ties do not weigh with Mr Deane in his transactions over the purchase of Dorlcote Mill: it is a good investment since its profits 'might be increased by the addition of steampower'. George Eliot's portrayal of an early capitalist arrangement, working through friends and relatives, appears to be historically accurate, since at this time the active owner-manager was more prominent than was to be the case later in the century. The change from the slow and painstaking accumulation of the Dodsons to the energy and calculated risk-taking of Guest and Co. or Mr Wakem enacts a crucial movement within the social milieu of St Ogg's. The novel enacts a moment of change which leaves none of the characters untouched.

There is in the portrayal of the Dodsons a richness of texture and detail which is both relevant and convincing. The domestic sanctities of Dodson life – their closets, linen and wills – are transmitted in the most thoroughgoing detail and with scrupulous balance. Thus, while Tom and Maggie are made miserable in visiting their Aunt Pullet, and have to wipe their feet on the second-best door-scraper, yet it is this very punctiliousness which later empowers Mrs Glegg to defend Maggie in her disgrace. The Dodson code, imaged and symbolized through keys, locks, closets, can only operate in a fixed and unchanging world, and can paradoxically only

55

triumph in death, through its funeral observances and its strict adherence to the laws of inheritance. The forces of change in St Ogg's in a sense bypass this mode. The novel takes place at a time of change in St Ogg's, and the transformation of society is set against a sense of an organic past. The newly motivating processes of law and economics are distinctly puzzling to the chief representative of that older organic community, Mr Tulliver. 'Everything winds about so – the more straightforrard you are, the more you're puzzled', he complains (p. 69). Tulliver is associated through imagery with a life of the outdoors, the mill, the river, horses, but he is dimly aware that this life is passing, and that, as he tells Mr Deane, the country 'could never again be what it used to be'. Deane's response is significant at this point, since he takes 'a more lively view of the present' (p. 133), and this lively view centres upon his hopes for technological change. The rhythm of life in St Ogg's is quickening. In one of his lectures to Tom, Mr Deane identifies the root cause: 'It's this steam, you see, that has made the difference – it drives on every wheel double pace and the wheel of Fortune along with 'em' (p. 507). As Deane and Wakem appreciate, capitalism is making great inroads on the traditional ways of life, and it is their characteristic ploy to put money to use, as do Tom and Bob Jakin in a smaller, imitative way.

The narrative of Maggie's growth and emotional education is carried on within a context of self-advancement, enterprise and litigation. While this progress, which leads away from the world represented by Dorlcote Mill, is felt as part of the evolution of society, there is a price to be paid. The choric voice of Dr Kenn, reflecting upon Maggie's downfall, articulates this sense of lost community most trenchantly:

'I should often lose heart at observing the want of fellowship and sen̂se of mutual responsibility among my own flock. At present everything seems tending towards the relaxation of ties – towards the substitution of wayward choice for the adherence to obligation which has its roots in the past.' (p. 625)

The statement is central, with its emphasis upon 'ties' and its condemnation of 'wayward choice'. Dr Kenn is here, perhaps, voicing not only Maggie's dilemma but that of the author herself, anxious to stress community and an organic way of life, yet at the same time defending the right and needs of the individual to evolve beyond that community. The note of disintegration in the novel itself is muted, however, and should not be over-stressed. The author makes it very clear that 'there is no private life untouched by a wider public life', and her sense of that interconnection is truly Wordsworthian in her emphasis upon communal and social ties. As so often in Wordsworth (George Eliot's favourite poet), that emphasis centres upon the role and function of memory: 'Life did change for Tom and Maggie; and yet they were not wrong in believing that the thoughts and loves of these first years would always make part of their lives' (p. 94). Memory binds the characters to the local and abiding; it is the countervailing principle of change which confronts them as they move away from the mill into individuality.

Under the effects of the bankruptcy, Tom stiffens and narrows into a mixture comprised of the loveless integrity of the Dodsons and the proud obstinacy of the Tullivers. Maggie, on the other hand, suffers constantly at the hands of others in the attempt to reconcile love with duty. She should not be simplistically seen as a passionate soul caught in the narrow confines of St Ogg's, since this is to make the creation of her character and relationships too diagrammatic. After the loss of the mill, Maggie strives to pursue the renunciatory way of Thomas à Kempis, although she regrets Philip Wakem's tempting art and culture. Both she and Tom lamentably lack that ready adaptability which marks those who survive best in St Ogg's, and which is comically epitomized by Bob Jakin's transformation from bargee and rat-catcher into packman and proto-capitalist. In later sections of the novel, it may be, Tom's faults in this respect are subjected to careful scrutiny while Maggie's are passed over or condoned.

Nevertheless, the society of St Ogg's, for all its provincial narrowness and humbug, is not destructive. It is rather Maggie's own imaginative and passionate inner life which plunges her into a series of crises. Society is responsible for her distress primarily in so far as she herself inwardly debates its values. The narrator's analysis of these 'dull men and women' on the banks of the Floss suggests that their 'oppressive narrowness' needs to be seen in relation to 'young natures in many generations, that in the onward tendency of human things have risen above the mental level of the generation before them' (p. 363). Yet the dullness against which Maggie rebels is not evil or squalid. On the contrary, the Dodsons have many redeeming features centring in their adherence to 'traditional duty or propriety' (p. 364). There are hidden benefits and qualities within this narrow life, and George Eliot at no place in the narrative seeks to sweep it away. The conflict within Maggie does not principally issue from the intractable self-righteousness of St Ogg's, but from the clash between her own romantic aspirations and her attachments to society, friends and family. Although Philip Wakem, as his name implies, awakens her to the deadening effects of provincialism, she remains attached to, rather than alienated from, that social context. The sexual, emotional and material gratifications which Stephen Guest offers are part of a genuine complex of temptations and needs, and are treated seriously. But such gratifications are counterbalanced by her fidelity to home and what is known, 'the sanctuary where sacred relics lay' (the religious language is significant here). Although 'St Ogg's passes judgment' upon her, in the second chapter of Book VII, Maggie has essentially pre-empted this process by her judgment upon herself. She cannot pass out of the life of St Ogg's, she tells Dr Kenn, for she would be bound to feel 'like a lonely wanderer – cut off from the past' (p. 626). She is ineluctably bound to the remembered people and places, and her decision to stay is vindicated by Philip's letter, Lucy's visit, and her renunciation of the possibilities opened up by Stephen's letter. Attachment to society, not alienation from it, remains the abiding note of the novel, and it is a society which can incorporate all the diverse elements of a period of transition. St Ogg's is subjected to careful analysis, since, as George Eliot remarks, 'no one class of persons or form of character is held up to reprobation or to exclusive admiration'. The characters, within the transforming processes of economics and history, are both free and determined by these processes.

The experiences provided for Maggie suggest that there may be a link in the novel's structure between intensity of feeling, which may be isolating, and impulses of sympathy and fellowship towards the ordinary community. Maggie suffers from the divisive effects of such education as she is given and obtains for herself, and she senses a growing gap between educated life and custom – the gap, for instance, between herself and her mother. In dramatizing these pressures, George Eliot addresses one of the central issues of the period. Her novels cover a critical period of transition, and frequently portray change as a sort of education. Maggie, through her experience, education and temperament, is sundered absolutely from her mother's world, and yet feels this sundering deeply and sadly. Education does not give her any upward mobility within a patriarchy. Literacy, in other words, carries within it here the seeds of her tragedy. Evolution could become a model for social change and advancement by showing how patterns could be traced in an evolving culture. Rapid social change, such as that witnessed by trade in St Ogg's, would begin to obliterate traditional areas of experience, ranging from spiritual and religious values to norms of work. Through her reading of Comte, Darwin and others, George Eliot was aware that change in a group, class or society was not explicable solely by reference to a monocausal external agency (steampower in St Ogg's, for instance). Internal factors are acting continuously to promote social and economic change, and personal structures of feeling alter to accommodate such changes. Forces of change in the social milieu of the novel are inevitable and critical for all the characters, and these forces act both externally and internally. Darwin at the same time insisted that nature operates gradually; it does not, he held, make leaps. Applied to the valley of the Floss, this might explain how factors such as industrialization, urbanization, literacy and occupational mobility would subtly alter value-systems, relationships and ultimately consciousness itself. These subtle alterations affect Tulliver and his daughter most dramatically, but are everywhere in play in the novel, as Mrs Glegg's disapproval of woven stockings comically demonstrates. The career of Mr Tulliver traces a declining graph between the economic axes of employer and dependant. His powerful and free-standing personality does not guarantee him any immunity to the forces of change to which his hasty nature exposes him too readily. Changing links of interdependence – Tom's connection with Deane, for instance, or Mrs Tulliver's with Lucy – will alter the balance of power in a community, with new constraints, but also with new options for the individual able to seize them, as Wakem or Deane, or even Bob Jakin, will do. In meditating on the fullness of the presentation of Tulliver or Maggie the reader may well reflect upon Marx's dictum that 'men make their own history, but they do not know that they are making it'.

In dramatizing these pressures and exploring these new developments for the individual, George Eliot virtually creates a new formal structure which was to extend the range of Victorian fiction. The constant interplay between community and isolation is finely caught at the end of the fifth chapter of Book III, where we are told how Maggie 'in her brown frock with her eyes reddened and her heavy hair pushed back' is 'a creature full of eager, passionate longings for all that was beautiful and glad: thirsty for all knowledge: with an ear straining after dreamy music that died away and would not come near to her' (p. 320). 'No wonder,' remarks the narrator, 'when there is this contrast between the outward and the inward, that painful collisions come of it' (ibid.). Nevertheless, the reader should resist too quick an endorsement of Philip Wakem's verdict that Maggie's life is a 'long suicide'. In Maggie's career, and in the cognate portrayal of Tom and Mr Tulliver, external incident and internal reactions are carefully integrated to reveal the moral standpoint of the author. The morality which illuminates Maggie's final decisive choice is to be seen as her highest point of moral development, while the moral attitudes of the society are largely determined by its physical and economic circumstances. Elements in the individual work against the determining properties of social conditioning to produce a realistic sense of a tragic action. The emphasis upon realism is especially to be noted. We do not find in George Eliot's work any of those wildly metaphoric characters in St Ogg's with which we may be familiar in Dickens. Rather, the pieces of the jigsaw which form a character are slowly built up and drawn together, the relationship of the character to others carefully delineated. Most important is the emphasis upon change: the central characters are felt to be undergoing processes of development and modification, just as the society also alters itself. While George Eliot does not dispense with the dramatic outer scene – as in the Red Deeps, the bazaar, the boating sequence, the flood itself – cause and effect are worked over and internalized with great artistry. The murders, marriages and lost wills of Victorian melodrama are abandoned in favour of a deeper and more real complexity of motive and feeling. That reality focuses in the unfolding of a life, rather than in the sudden and arbitrary ending, and the river Floss may justly be taken as authorial metaphor for the endless flow of time through history and for that sense of Maggie as one of those 'delicate vessels' which carry forward 'through the ages the treasure of human affections', as George Eliot expressed it in *Daniel Deronda*.

In order to define the atmosphere of her novel, in the first chapter of Book I V George Eliot interrupts the narration in order to juxtapose two different orders of 'reality', the imposing castles on the Rhine and the ruined villages of the Rhône (pp. 361–2). The Rhenish castles fill the beholder with a sense of 'poetry' because they are surviving monuments of a 'grand historic life', while the 'ugly, grovelling existence' of the Rhône seems to be echoed in life on the Floss, with its concomitant 'oppressive narrowness' (p. 363). Yet it is just this narrowness and oppression we need to feel if we are to comprehend the 'suffering, whether of martyr or victim, which belongs to every historical advance of mankind' (ibid.). The flow of the river images this historical tide, and indeed it is this seminal image which first confronts the reader:

A wide plain, where the broadening Floss hurries on between its green banks to the sea, and the loving tide, rushing to meet it, checks its passage with an impetuous embrace. (p. 53)

The history of the Dodsons and Tullivers is placed securely within the greater flow of nature and history, and their individual histories contribute to that 'mighty tide' (ibid.). Indeed, the broad movement counteracted by the impetuosity of the tidal current neatly images the distinctions between the two families. In moving from the river to the 'unresting' mill-wheel on the Ripple, the narrator transfers from one significant image – the river of life – to another – the wheel of fortune. It is upon this wheel that the characters are tossed and turned: 'Mr Deane had been advancing in the world as rapidly as Mr Tulliver had been going down in it' (p. 286).

Through this cyclic emphasis, the novelist creates her effects of contrast and balance, and this notion is most fully explored in the pairing of Tom and Maggie. The setting and tone of the narrative help in conferring upon the impulses of the passionate heroine some of the significance and weight of tragedy. When, for instance, Maggie pushes Lucy into the mud:

> There were passions at war in Maggie at that moment to have made a tragedy, if tragedies were made by passion only. (p. 164)

The passage is subtly representative: Maggie is prey to that rashness of spirit which will ruin her adult life. She does not, in a sense, adapt to her circumstances, and this is a ruling idea throughout the novel. Thus in the opening conversation about Tom's education, the reader is aware that Mr Tulliver is more far-sighted than Mrs Tulliver. Yet none of them is able to cope with the world of Deane and Wakem. Each character is exposed through his or her reaction to the fact of change, but it is a change only the narrator can fully encompass:

> Life did change for Tom and Maggie; and yet they were not wrong in believing that the thoughts and loves of these first years would always make part of their lives. (p. 94)

The inevitability of change, and the failure to respond to it, may lead towards tragedy (or comedy). George Eliot structures the book into two movements, each with a tragic outcome: first, the downfall of Mr Tulliver, ending at Book V; second, the careers of his children. Although the principal motif of *The Mill on the Floss* is that of growth, the countervailing movement in the first part is of Mr Tulliver's failure. The story of Tulliver authentically embodies some of the principles of contrast upon which George Eliot has constructed her narrative: parents against children, Dodsons against Tullivers, brother against sister, husband against wife, St Ogg's against the mill. Yet the most fundamental divisions lie within the man himself. Pride leads him into entanglements with the law, his friends, neighbours and rivals, and his catastrophe grows organically out of his own character. In this sense it is absolutely just to observe that 'Character is fate'. Tragedy in literature is usually said to define the way tragic heroes are responsible for what happens to them, and only gradually wake up to a realization of their own faults. We may wish to make a distinction here between disaster, which happens outside oneself, and tragedy, which comes from within, and this idea may illuminate our reading of the ending of the whole novel. Tragedy cannot be accidental; it must have a feeling of inevitability. While Mr Tulliver lives in a universe which is quite indifferent to him, and sometimes seems to suffer at the hands of fate, the miller contributes largely to his own downfall. It is often

61

said that pride characterizes the tragic hero, and certainly a kind of pride does mark Tulliver's career. This pride and the other parts of his character, his firmness and inability to compromise, make Tulliver a tragic figure. Like other tragic protagonists, Mr Tulliver contrasts with the reality or ordinariness of the world about him, and makes repeated mistakes in his relations with that world. From his mistaken choice of wife, his desire for a gentleman's education for Tom, his legal battle with Pivart, and his desire to repay Mrs Glegg, to his bankruptcy, fight with Wakem and subsequent death, the failings of Mr Tulliver's career are intimately bound up with his positive qualities as a man. While Mr Deane, for example, coolly appraises Wakem as a man of business, Tulliver angrily boasts that he will never let 'anybody get hold of his whip-hand' (p. 90), only to have finally to allow that very thing to happen. Once regarded as a poor matrimonial prospect, Mr Deane rises to a position of eminence through engagement in, and understanding of, commerce. The contrast is in some ways similar to that which Hardy was to make between Henchard and Farfrae in *The Mayor of Casterbridge*. As Deane explains to Tom, he does not 'find fault with the change', because trade leads the world to 'use its wits at inventions of one sort or other' (p. 507). Tulliver loses control of the mill through litigation over water rights, while Deane places his trust in steampower. The working relations obtaining at the mill are in a sense still feudally based. The link between Tulliver and Luke allows for co-operation and human feeling; in the newer sphere of business at St Ogg's relations are dominated by competition (Deane and Wakem) and accumulation (the Dodsons). We should be on our guard against an overly schematic reading of the novel in relation to Tulliver's downfall, and of making a simple contrast between Dorlcote Mill and St Ogg's. Nevertheless, it is clear that Mr Tulliver (and Mrs Moss) head for ruin, some of it self-inflicted, while the more rational citizens of the town thrive and increase. The structural role of Mr Tulliver's downfall lies in the parallels George Eliot hints at with Maggie's career, and many of those enforced parallels can be most fully illuminated by the student paying some careful attention to the feminist issues raised by her case.

The Feminist Perspective

The Mill on the Floss gives sympathetic consideration to the plight of an intelligent young woman striving to overcome narrow and restrictive social circumstances. Her contact with people outside that society – the gypsies, for instance – is significantly painful, since she is humiliated and has to flee back to the family circle. It has been interestingly suggested that the gypsy women are some kind of secret 'double' for Maggie, a secret self she can never become. There is certainly in the novel a studied opposition between stereotypes: female feeling and passion set against male authority and repression. In this particularized society law is defined in terms of paternal preference: Mr Tulliver owns the mill by virtue of one hundred years of family possession. Patrimonial property rights are intimately connected with paternal male authority and privilege, aspects of maleness which are neatly mirrored in Tom's behaviour and attitudes. Mary Ann Evans's ambivalent position as mistress of her father's house at Griff, and her rebellion and contrition over church-going, were an apt initiation for the young writer into the limits circumscribing 'the woman's place'. These emotional patterns of early adulthood left a mark upon this highly autobiographical novel. Mr Tulliver is, of course, not a stereotypically 'heavy' Victorian father. He loves Maggie deeply, and she turns to him repeatedly in crises. His role as disciplinarian is, as it were, transferred on to Tom, who becomes the lawgiver. Maggie is thus made to internalize male norms of behaviour, to seek approval and to avoid conflict and assertion. But she cannot gain this approval; the Dodsons' rule-oriented codes of behaviour are outraged by her appearance and her actions. She and Philip are equally outcast and abnormal in a society which is exclusively male in outlook. Mr Tulliver has selected his wife because she was 'a bit weak', just as Stephen Guest will later select Lucy because she was 'a little darling'. The central brother–sister relationship reinforces all these stereotypes, and Tom is always able to dominate Maggie by threatening to withdraw his affection.

The question of woman throwing off oppressive institutionalization in favour of finding her 'self' is made more difficult by the realization that 'individuality' is hard to define except in relation to a social group. At the opening of the novel Maggie is framed in a distant perspective, and is to be named by her parents. She is part of a community, yet part of her cannot fit into this community, the part of her which is most 'female'. The narrator remarks that Maggie's life was a struggle located 'almost entirely within her own soul, one shadowy army fighting another', while Tom is 'engaged in a dustier, noisier warfare, grappling with more substantial obstacles, and gaining more definite conquests' (p. 405). Both Tulliver offspring struggle, but for Tom there is an outer sphere to struggle with, unavailable to women. Maggie can only feel superior to Tom in her capacity for suffering, which 'No true boy feels' (p. 348) – again, a sidelong glance at Philip is implied here. The novel therefore addresses problems inherent in belonging to groups in order to attain identity, and the muddle which Maggie experiences at the crisis is specifically a crisis of belonging which could never afflict Tom or Stephen. Each of the men in the novel – Mr Tulliver, Tom, Philip, Stephen – represents a masculinity which could only respond to part of Maggie's nature, a nature which can never find its true expression within this patriarchy. Tom, a self-made man, is enabled to regain the mill through his active career at Guest and Co.; Maggie's only possibility is self-exile. Only at the moment of the flood are the sex-roles reversed, and equality momentarily attained through the ending.

The Dodsons have shown us (and Maggie) that the female role of suffering and passivity can become trivialized and feeble, as when Mrs Pullet indulges in her bouts of public mourning, an act as ornamental as her bracelets and 'architectural bonnet' (p. 112). Through such progressive trivialization the female nature may be perverted into a permanent role of pointless suffering, such as Mrs Tulliver indulges in after the bankruptcy. The only other role model available to Maggie is the pliantly obedient Lucy, whom she angrily pushed into the mud. The primary phase of Maggie's 'education in womanhood' leads her to reject these role models of her immediate circle. She begins to long for education, and at the schoolmaster's realizes she could gain more from this education than Tom. The conversation at this point, however, shows the dangers of such aspiration:

> 'Girls can't do Euclid: can they, sir?'
> 'They can pick up a little of everything, I daresay,' said Mr Stelling. 'They've a great deal of superficial cleverness: but they couldn't go far into anything. They're quick and shallow.'
> Tom, delighted with this verdict, telegraphed his triumph by wagging his head at Maggie behind Mr Stelling's chair. As for Maggie, she had hardly ever been so mortified: she had been so proud to be called 'quick' all her little life, and now it appeared that this quickness was the brand of inferiority. It would have been better to be slow, like Tom. (pp. 220–21)

This significant exchange delineates a society in which women must accept their place. Maggie's mother had been 'healthy, fair, plump, and dull-witted, in short, the flower of her family for beauty and amiability' (p. 62). The woman's duties, as she conceives them, centre around her home and family possessions, her elder-flower wine, clothes and linens. These Dodson pieties form an important part of Maggie's character also, so that in rebelling against them she also rebels against part of herself. Yet her devastating 'need of being loved' (p. 89) allows Tom to dominate her throughout, and her rebellious hair-cutting is met with 'a chorus of reproach and derision' (p. 125), as is her later flight with Stephen. George Eliot wrote to a friend, 'We women are always in danger of living too exclusively in the affections', and it is not a danger which Maggie, baulked of education or career, successfully avoids. Mr Wakem's trenchant comment, 'We don't ask what a woman does, we ask whom she belongs to' (pp. 542–3), aptly defines the magnitude of Maggie's problems here. Her only available vocation is to love, and this desire runs counter to what Philip terms her 'wrong ideas of self-conquest' (p. 436). Philip is himself compromised and self-interested in his analysis at this juncture, and both he and Maggie seem insecure in their sexual identities throughout the Red Deeps section. It may be argued, indeed, that in the imagery and landscapes of these interviews the narrative reveals more than it purports to know about sexual nature and role-playing.

In considering the nature of this range of image and reference it is worth noting that, in the portrayal of Maggie, George Eliot is drawing upon a kind of running subtext which relates to conventions of the literary heroine within nineteenth-century literature. Indeed, Maggie herself makes this clear when she explains to Philip Wakem why she cannot finish the reading of Madame de Staël's *Corinne*:

> 'I didn't finish the book,' said Maggie. 'As soon as I came to the blond-haired young lady reading in the park, I shut it up and determined to read no further. I foresaw that that light complexioned girl would win away all the love from Corinne and make her miserable. I'm determined to read no more books where the blond haired women carry away all the happiness. I should begin to have a prejudice against them –'   (pp. 432–3)

This exchange in the Red Deeps expresses a fundamental sexual conflict in the novel between dark and light, a polarity centred of course in the descriptions of Maggie and Lucy. The modern reader needs to be alert to a naturalized literary symbolism here, and to the significance of Philip's supposition that Maggie 'will avenge the dark women in [her] own person: carry away all the love from your cousin Lucy' (p. 433). From the moment when Maggie pushes Lucy into the mud the covert rivalry between women is a potent underlying force in the text, a force which culminates in Maggie's (unwitting) act of carrying away 'all the love' from her rival. When Maggie told Philip she wished 'to avenge Rebecca and Flora Mac-Ivor and Minna' (ibid.), and returned de Staël's *Corinne* unfinished, the Victorian reader would immediately pick up the references to the dark-haired heroines of romance tradition in Scott's fiction and elsewhere. It may be no accident that Corinne's successful blonde rival was named Lucy, nor that Minna in *The Pirate* has a fair-haired sister who is cheerful and well behaved. The romance pattern formulated by Scott characteristically figured a triangular relationship in which dark and fair heroines vied for the affections of the hero. In the characterization of Stephen Guest, in particular, it may be that George Eliot reverts too closely to the heroic type of romance fiction. However that may be, it needs to be observed that in *The Mill on the Floss* the emotional entanglements depicted find their source in the highly stylized genre of romance, upon which the author imposes the disciplines of Victorian realism. The conflict between dark and fair (repeated with Dorothea and Celia Brooke in *Middlemarch*), and the denouement on the Floss, are the most notable residue of George Eliot's exposure to romance fiction. The drowning may be the final expiation or renunciation of the desire for a kind of revenge on Lucy's idealized and glamourized version of womanliness, and it is an act which neatly counterbalances the earlier push into the water of the pond.

These crucial exchanges with Philip take place in the Red Deeps, a locale whose name is redolent with sexual overtones. This is a place of 'very capricious hollows and mounds' (p. 392) in which Maggie first comes to recognize herself as a sexual creature. Colour and landscape function powerfully as sexual referents here, recalling Freud's remark that the 'complicated topography of the female genital parts makes one understand how it is that they are often represented as landscapes'. It is within this topography that Maggie feels torn between brother and lover, and between the pulls of pleasure, guilt and renunciation.

Following upon her pitying love for Philip, Maggie awakens into more self-consciously sexual life in her encounter with Stephen Guest. The problematic nature of this episode needs to be looked at in detail, but in reminding ourselves of the powerful if muffled feminist strain in the novel it may be useful to glance at Maggie's dream of St Ogg. In the dream, Maggie, sailing downstream with Stephen, sees St Ogg rowing the Virgin, who turns out to be Lucy. The saint himself is first of all revealed as Tom, and then transforms himself mysteriously into Philip. Reaching out towards him Maggie capsizes their own boat and begins to sink. The content of the dream here suggests powerfully enough to the reader the nature of Maggie's guilt at what she feels is her irresponsibility, and even the deeper notion that both Tom and Philip seek, in their different ways, to subvert and control her inner nature. Through the dream, it may be, George Eliot suggests that intensity of inner life can be ultimately destructive. The narrator (and the reader) pursues Maggie's career from the fantasy-centred life of the child who reacts to a variety of criticisms and deprivations, through the adolescent fantasies generated by culture and sex, towards the denouement. In the course of this depicted career the narrator is especially pertinacious in tracing, through the varied 'narratives' which Maggie tells herself, her own versions of reality. Each area of her fantasy life, even when it is rejected, leaves its imprint upon her changing sense of self. In literary terms her taking up and rejection of Scott and romantic literature, or of Thomas à Kempis and renunciation, leave traces within the maturing heroine which emerge at the crisis on the river with Stephen Guest. It may be that the consolatory and escapist provisions of literary fantasy return with a vengeance in the flood scene. The literary elements in Maggie's formation are scrupulously tied in with the heroine's devotion to habit and nostalgia, those things which Maggie says 'my past life has made dear to me', and yet the romantic strand in her make-up clashes unwittingly with this passion for the past. There is perhaps a dislocation in the text between the powerful forces of nature which are released finally and arbitrarily and the binding loyalties of the past to which Maggie emotionally adheres. The reader is left to decide whether Maggie's powers and potentialities are lost to the narrow community of the Floss, apart from acting as a focus of nostalgia for a handful of survivors of her tragic life.

The Crisis

Stephen Guest is not a character who appears in the solidly realized and leisurely early sections of the book, and his sudden appearance has been the subject of some critical disagreement. Initially, it may be, he makes a disagreeable impression upon us:

the fine young man who is leaning down from his chair to snap the scissors in the extremely abbreviated face of the 'King Charles' lying on the young lady's feet, is no other than Mr Stephen Guest, whose diamond ring, attar of roses, and air of nonchalant leisure at twelve o'clock in the day are the graceful and odoriferous result of the largest oil-mill and the most extensive wharf in St Ogg's.   (p. 469)

The reader needs to determine whether the character improves from this unpromising beginning. Certainly George Eliot does not wish us to view him as a dandified trifler with female emotion like Hardy's Alec d'Urberville. At the same time the catalogue of qualities which leads him to choose Lucy as his wife reveals a self-regarding element in the young man which George Eliot carefully foregrounds. He 'approved his own choice of her', we are told, 'chiefly because she did not strike him as a remarkable rarity' (p. 477). The blandness suggested here is pointed up in the following chapter, when Stephen first encounters Lucy's opposite, the dark and striking figure of Maggie. While the entanglement between the two has always been a source of critical remark, it is worth pointing out that their

67

relationship does offer a balance to the heroine's earlier friendship with Philip, a friendship which is founded upon pity and mutual cultural interests, but is fatally lacking in sexual attraction. Maggie, in the later stages of the book, is indeed on the horns of a dilemma: both the relationships depend upon making a moral choice which will lead her towards self-sacrifice and possible self-mutilation. She is to some extent existing only within the roles defined for her by the various ideals and desires of Philip or Stephen. In the great boating scene, George Eliot beautifully distinguishes between the feelings of the pair of lovers: Stephen is half aware that he has rowed past Luckreth, where they were to meet Lucy, while Maggie has suspended her will and motivation. It is the release into half-willing passion which must cause Maggie's crisis at this point. It seems here as if the stresses and dependency of childhood will never allow her to bring together different strands of her own personality to form a coherent sense of selfhood. The narrator's description aptly mimes out for us in the language and rhythm of the text the contrasting inner elements:

> They glided rapidly along, to Stephen's rowing, helped by the backward-flowing tide, past the Tofton trees and houses – on between the silent, sunny fields and pastures which seemed filled with a natural joy that had no reproach for theirs. The breath of the young, unwearied day, the delicious rhythmic dip of the oars, the fragmentary song of a passing bird heard now and then as if it were only the overflowing of brim-full gladness, the sweet solitude of a twofold consciousness that was mingled into one by that grave untiring gaze which need not be averted – what else could there be in their minds for the first hour? (p. 589)

This crucial passage embodies in fictional form some of the ideas about sexuality which Freud was soon to formulate. In particular the erotic urge, the pleasure principle, is felt by Maggie to be in contention with some outside or 'higher' voice which we may identify in Freudian terms as the super-ego, the deeply ingrained parental voice. The restrictions embodied in this parental voice are gradually taken into the growing personality in an unconscious process of repression to form what Freud calls the reality principle. The reality principle allows the person to survive in the external world, but at the cost of repression, as Maggie now discovers. Freud wrote that 'heavy restrictions upon sexual life are unavoidable' if civilization is to be maintained, and he went on to argue for a close and inextricable connection between *Eros*, the life instinct, and *Thanatos*, the death instinct. In rejecting the pleasures of sexuality, it may be, Maggie unconsciously seizes upon the related death-urge which finds its satisfaction in the flood. Once full realization of her moral position dawns upon Maggie she acts in consistency with her past, the whole process and meaning of development and growth which the novel has so carefully traced out. The claims which Stephen urges, claims of passion, are here based on a circular argument, and he cannot sustain this against other claims which insist on their primacy within Maggie. What the reader must decide is whether Maggie is making herself an object of sacrifice or satisfying her inmost needs:

'Maggie,' he said, at last, pausing before her, and speaking in a tone of imploring wretchedness. 'Have some pity – hear me – forgive me for what I did yesterday. I will obey you now – I will do nothing without your full consent. But don't blight our lives for ever by a rash perversity that can answer no good purpose to any one – that can only create new evils. Sit down, dearest – wait – think what you are going to do. Don't treat me as if you couldn't trust me.'

He had chosen the most effective appeal; but Maggie's will was fixed unswervingly on the coming wrench. She had made up her mind to suffer.

'We must not wait,' she said, in a low but distinct voice. 'We must part at once.'

'We *can't* part, Maggie,' said Stephen, more impetuously. 'I can't bear it. What is the use of inflicting that misery on me?'   (p. 600)

This is complex, and there is a web of interrelated claims which muddles the polarities of Maggie's determination to suffer, and Stephen's egotistical 'I can't bear it'. In a sense, every incident of Maggie's formative years has led towards this moment of decision. But it may be that those incidents have created a character incapable of true and independent choice. The room for manoeuvre for the women of St Ogg's is strictly circumscribed, so that Maggie can discern no viable alternatives to life with Stephen or life back in the town. What the novel explores here is the idea of worthwhile sacrifice, and many of these notions are put more clearly in the disinterested ruminations of Dr Kenn, though when he suggests that 'the idea of an ultimate marriage between Stephen and Maggie' is to be seen as the 'least evil' (p. 627) we should once more remind ourselves that this is still an overwhelmingly masculine society. The narrator instructs us at this point that the 'great problem of the shifting relation between passion and duty is clear to no man who is capable of apprehending it' (p. 627), an oracular dictum which gingerly treads the maze linking Freud's pleasure and reality principles. Maggie would seem in this great dilemma to be caught in a vacillating curve between her sense of self and her sense of others, notably Philip Wakem, Lucy and her brother, a curve which she can identify as the clash between duty and impulse. Her 'last conflict' involves the pleading letter from Stephen Guest, and its rejection in favour of those 'memories that no passion could long quench' (p. 648). Memories work in Maggie as feelings towards others. She is, perhaps, deeply divided within herself, and her renunciation may seem a perverse form of selfishness. The Maggie who surrenders to impulse is given to us from the start of the novel, in her cutting off her hair, pushing Lucy into the mud, and running away to the gypsies. Against this, and the temptations of Stephen's letter, she picks up à Kempis once more, but the moment of rejection and renunciation is obliterated by the flood which finally restores a sense of certainty to her life. Maggie has been unsympathetically described as 'monstrous' in turning into an 'angel of renunciation'. While this perhaps distorts the feeling and implications of the text, there is a serious discrepancy between her motives towards joy and self-punishment. It has been aptly observed that there is a correlation between the floods of feeling which associate her with the river and the way in which crushing and grinding processes associate Tom with the mill. The mill to which she finally returns may, for all its homely qualities, be taken as a symbol of the male sphere of honour and work. If brother and sister are 'not divided' in death, as their epitaph claims, the truth is that concepts of gender difference divide them radically in life, and also serve to divide Maggie within herself. That gender difference relates to a patriarchal society and to a patriarchal art-form, the novel. We may only speculate on the inner psychological cost of Mary Ann Evans's deliberate abnegation of femaleness in her transformation to the 'male' authorial voice of 'George Eliot'. One of the elements in the flood scene may be a subconscious desire to drown the dominant male father figure under the guise of rescue and reconciliation with the brother. Being female in provincial England in the Victorian age, the novel indicates, is a supremely determining experience. Yet it is part of the fascination of the book that George Eliot appears simultaneously to endorse and subvert the norm of patriarchal dominance.

The Tragic Ending

The tragic ending of *The Mill on the Floss* has proved critically contentious, 'a tardy expedient for the solution of Maggie's difficulties', as Henry James succinctly expressed it. This 'dishonest contrivance' (Joan Bennett), composed by a suspiciously tearful George Eliot, arises out of 'self-pity' and 'self-idealisation' (Leavis) on the part of the author, so it is claimed. Maggie's 'senseless sacrifice' (Knoepflmacher) is the ruination of the novel through its 'arbitrary tragic ending' (Walter Allen). There is clearly some justice in this widespread feeling. Freud argued cogently that the fundamental problem for art is the universalizing, displacement and concealing of the private wish-fulfilment of the creative artist, in order that the reader may adequately and successfully 'receive' that wish-fulfilment. In the flood scene, it may be alleged, George Eliot did not fully carry out that process of depersonalization of the text. An awareness of the mode of tragedy deployed in the novel, however, may help us to a more sympathetic understanding of George Eliot's aims and intentions here. Tragedy arises in George Eliot's world when major characters 'in the onward tendency of things' rise above the general level of humanity while remaining tied to them 'by the strongest fibres of their hearts'. The novel presents and dramatizes a society which is materialistic and narrow-minded, and against which the Tulliver passions struggle fatally in both generations. A review of *The Mill on the Floss* in 1860 likened its effects to those of ancient Greek tragedy, and the central doctrine of those plays, the responsibility of individuals for their own actions, is certainly present in both Mr Tulliver and Maggie.

A reviewer of *Felix Holt* in 1866 remarked, 'George Eliot's novels are not novels in the ordinary sense of the term – they are really dramas.' Certainly George Eliot does utilize such an Aristotelian notion as *hamartia* (the tragic flaw) to show how her protagonists are led through their emotions to struggle against the overruling power of causation, what she called in *The Spanish Gypsy* 'The Dire strife/Of poor humanity's afflicted will,/Struggling in vain with ruthless destiny'. The 'destiny' is to be understood in her world, not as something imposed by the gods, but as the network of cause and effect which leads to what she called 'various conditions of mutual dependence'. The lawgiver in her universe is nothing other than cause and effect, and it is up to people to discover and foresee the operations of this law, and to act according to the duties disclosed through this law. That is why so many of her characters are faced with crucial choice, a choice often imaged as a choice of paths. It is that choice which Maggie to some extent postpones by the involuntary act of floating away on the water. The characters cannot ever evade choice. Mr Tulliver resolves not to borrow money from a client of Wakem's, yet within weeks he has done so. Tulliver relies foolhardily upon 'unassisted intellect' to arrive at 'questionable conclusions', yet he remains a truly tragic figure. Unlike the tragedy discussed by Aristotle, George Eliot's art is essentially democratic: as she remarks, the 'pride and obstinacy of millers, and other insignificant people ... have their tragedy'. Because she was suspicious of the highly plotted novels of Dickens and Wilkie Collins, George Eliot stressed that tragedy stems from character and incident. It is in the nature of her protagonists that they cannot accurately foresee consequence, like Maggie 'stepping always by a peculiar gift in the muddiest places' (p. 92). The novelist had observed in *Adam Bede* that the 'noblest nature' is often

71

'the most blinded'; such protagonists lack well-regulated minds and are perhaps the more likeable for that. Certainly, in the moral continuum of her novels such people as Tulliver and Maggie are to be set against those who live for 'a prudent calculation of results'. The Dodsons, with their accurate prediction of cause and effect, declare that 'if trouble's sent ... it isn't sent without a cause' (p. 287). Against this utilitarian calculus is set the 'magnificent futility' of the Tulliver strain.

Within such a context of moral considerations Maggie must adopt one of two courses. She may either adapt to the mode of life of those around her or live out the implications of feelings which are constantly at odds with her family circle. Darwin had shown that organisms were only successfully able to survive through adaptation; for Maggie, as for her father, this proves a 'puzzlin' world'. In the presentation of both their characters George Eliot stresses the note of conflict, and places great emphasis upon polarity in a metaphor which links the mental and geographical landscapes of the Floss valley:

> And the present time was like the level plain where men lose their belief in volcanoes and earthquakes, thinking to-morrow will be as yesterday and the giant forces that used to shake the earth are for ever laid to sleep. (p. 184)

In such a passage we may silently refer to the contrast in character between the 'level plain' of the mental landscape of the quietly accumulating Dodsons and the 'volcanoes and earthquakes', which typify the Tullivers' relationship with their milieu. Such volcanic outbursts may only lead to tragedy, and they are internalized in the portrayal of Maggie, for instance, in the Red Deeps, where 'one has a sense of uneasiness in looking at her – a sense of opposing elements, of which a fierce collision is imminent' (p. 394). That 'fierce collision' focuses itself upon Stephen Guest, and the only calm which is vouchsafed the tragic heroine here is the calm of death, the oblivion of the watery finale.

The classical tragic feeling is complicated by George Eliot's highly Victorian concern with free will and determinism, and by the formal difficulties of handling a tragic action in a realist form like the novel. Maggie as an individual is, it may be said, rarely enabled to choose her path freely, because she is always vulnerable and needs urgently to cultivate her own inner life. Tragedy arises partly out of circumstances, but more powerfully (as Bradley was to suggest of Shakespearian tragedy) out of inner conflict, what George Eliot characterizes as 'that partial, divided action of our nature which makes half the tragedy of the human lot'. Character is a matter of choice: 'we prepare ourselves for sudden deeds by the reiterated choice of good or evil which gradually determines character.' The female situation with its enforced passivity and stultification does not allow free choice, but it is clear that the heart of the novel rests upon an antagonism between rival claims and value-systems. The internal conflicts in the heroine are expressed as in Shakespearian tragedy by outward circumstance. Maggie's error lies perhaps in her impulsive nature, yet we respect her faults more than Tom's self-righteousness. A tragic hero may be destroyed from within by qualities which are not inherently bad, and George Eliot joins to this ancient notion that post-Darwinian perception that survival of the fittest does not mean survival of the best people in St Ogg's. The need for closure in the narrative, for resolution of the problems, was largely determined by the nature of the reading audiences for whom George Eliot wrote. For a variety of reasons, therefore, she was compelled to truncate the finely observed process of growth in Maggie towards maturity. In picturing the river as an image of the flux of time and change, and the flood as an emblem of human helplessness in nature, George Eliot was working fully within the tragic mode. Imposing closure on development through the tragic ending also allows George Eliot to impose formal closure of narrative expectations – the reader feels satisfied that life has been given a coherent shape and comprehensible pattern.

The individual reader must decide, finally, what the response to the flood scene may be. It has been well said that fictional endings create more tensions than they resolve, and this may be the case in *The Mill on the Floss*. Readers would do well to feel their way back through the intricacies, and fidelity to experience, of the whole narrative. If we do this we may feel less ready than some critics to dismiss the ending as arbitrary wish-fulfilment. Art, George Eliot held, should extend the human capacity for sympathy and understanding. *The Mill on the Floss*, whatever is locally problematic in the text, triumphantly justifies that belief.

Select Bibliography

Biographical

GORDON S. HAIGHT *George Eliot*, Oxford University Press, 1968: the standard biography.

RUBY V. REDINGER *The Emergent Self*, Bodley Head, 1975: a more psychological account of the author's life and thought.

Background of ideas

JOHN HOLLOWAY *The Victorian Sage*, Archon, 1953, Chapter 5: relates ideas to technique.

BERNARD J. PARIS *Experiments in Life*, Wayne State University Press, 1965: an advanced study which relates the novels to George Eliot's ideas.

THOMAS PINNEY (ed.) *Essays of George Eliot*, Routledge and Kegan Paul, 1963.

SALLY SHUTTLEWORTH *George Eliot and Nineteenth Century Science*, Cambridge University Press, 1984.

BASIL WILLEY *Nineteenth Century Studies*, Penguin Books, 1973, Chapter 8: a useful description of George Eliot's intellectual context.

Critical studies

WALTER ALLEN *George Eliot*, Weidenfeld and Nicolson, 1965, pp. 106–17.

CATHERINE BELSEY *Critical Practice*, Methuen, 1980, pp. 67–84: a penetrating analysis of 'classic realism' in fiction of the period.

JOAN BENNETT *George Eliot*, Cambridge University Press, 1962, Chapter 6: a mature judicious commentary.

JEROME BUCKLEY *Season of Youth*, Harvard University Press, 1974, Chapter 4: discusses the novel as *Bildungsroman* (novel of development).

DAVID CARROLL (ed.) *George Eliot: The Critical Heritage*, Routledge and Kegan Paul, 1971.

GEORGE R. CREEGER (ed.) *George Eliot: A Collection of Critical Essays*, Prentice-Hall, 1970.

R. P. DRAPER (ed.) *'The Mill on the Floss' and 'Silas Marner'*,

Casebook Series, Macmillan, 1977: an invaluable collection of critical material on the novel.

GORDON S. HAIGHT and R. T. VAN ARSDEL (eds.) *George Eliot: A Centenary Tribute*, Macmillan, 1982.

BARBARA HARDY *The Novels of George Eliot*, Athlone Press, 1959: a subtle study of George Eliot's handling of form and viewpoint.
Particularities, Peter Owen, 1982, Chapter 3: a suggestive reading of the novel which incorporates a plausible defence of the ending.

BARBARA HARDY (ed.) *Critical Essays on George Eliot*, Routledge and Kegan Paul, 1970.

W. J. HARVEY *The Art of George Eliot*, Chatto and Windus, 1961: a significant essay on tone and form in the novels.

R. T. JONES *George Eliot*, Cambridge University Press, 1970, Chapter 3.

JEANNETTE KING *Tragedy in the Victorian Novel*, Cambridge University Press, 1978, Chapter 4: discusses the novel as formal tragedy.

U. C. KNOEPFLMACHER *George Eliot's Early Novels*, University of California Press, 1968, Chapter 6: a valuable discussion of the interweaving of romantic, realistic and tragic strands in the novel.

F. R. LEAVIS *The Great Tradition*, Penguin Books, 1972, pp. 52–60: a brief but seminal statement about authorial involvement with the heroine.

T. S. PEARCE *George Eliot*, Evans, 1973, Chapter 6.

JEROME THALE *The Novels of George Eliot,* Columbia University Press, 1959, Chapter 2: a sound analysis of the social aspects of the novel.

A. E. S. VINER *George Eliot*, Oliver and Boyd, 1971, Chapter 2.

RAYMOND WILLIAMS *The English Novel*, Paladin, 1974, Chapter 3: an important critique of George Eliot's attitudes towards community and history.

Feminist perspectives

NINA AUERBACH *Woman and the Demon*, Harvard University Press, 1982.

PATRICIA BEER *Reader, I Married Him*, Macmillan, 1974, Chapter 5.

JENNI CALDER *Women and Marriage in Victorian Fiction*, Thames and Hudson, 1976.

SANDRA GILBERT and SUSAN GUBAR *The Madwoman in the Attic*, Yale University Press, 1979, Chapter 14.

Masterstudies: The Mill on the Floss

DIANNE SADOFF *Monsters of Affection*, Johns Hopkins University Press, 1982, Chapter 2.

ELAINE SHOWALTER *A Literature of Their Own*, Virago, 1978, Chapter 4.

PATRICIA MEYER SPACKS *The Female Imagination*, Allen and Unwin, 1976.

MORE ABOUT PENGUINS, PELICANS AND PUFFINS

For further information about books available from Penguins please write to Dept EP, Penguin Books Ltd, Harmondsworth, Middlesex UB7 0DA.

In the U.S.A.: For a complete list of books available from Penguins in the United States write to Dept DG, Penguin Books, 299 Murray Hill Parkway, East Rutherford, New Jersey 07073.

In Canada: For a complete list of books available from Penguins in Canada write to Penguin Books Canada Ltd, 2801 John Street, Markham, Ontario L3R 1B4.

In Australia: For a complete list of books available from Penguins in Australia write to the Marketing Department, Penguin Books Australia Ltd, P.O. Box 257, Ringwood, Victoria 3134.

In New Zealand: For a complete list of books available from Penguins in New Zealand write to the Marketing Department, Penguin Books (N.Z.) Ltd, Private Bag, Takapuna, Auckland 9.

In India: For a complete list of books available from Penguins in India write to Penguin Overseas Ltd, 706 Eros Apartments, 56 Nehru Place, New Delhi 110019.

THE PENGUIN ENGLISH LIBRARY

GEORGE ELIOT

ADAM BEDE

EDITED BY STEPHEN GILL

Adam Bede, George Eliot's first full-length novel, richly celebrates the long-vanished world of the rural community. Yet it is more than merely a charming pastoral, for it tells the story of tragically interlocking human destinies, of the seduction which destroys the young life of Hetty Sorrel and of the suffering which shapes Adam Bede into manhood.

THE MILL ON THE FLOSS

EDITED BY A. S. BYATT

Published in 1860, George Eliot's *The Mill on the Floss* has a strong autobiographical element which is reflected in her vivid portrayal of childhood and adolescence in mid-nineteenth-century England. This is one of George Eliot's best-loved works containing an affectionate and perceptive study of provincial life, a brilliant evocation of the complexities of human relationships and a heroine whose rebellious spirit closely resembles George Eliot's own.

and

DANIEAL DERONDA
EDITED BY BARBARA HARDY
FELIX HOLT
EDITED BY PETER COVENEY
MIDDLEMARCH
EDITED BY W. J. HARVEY
ROMOLA
EDITED BY ANDREW SAUNDERS
SCENES OF CLERICAL LIFE
EDITED BY DAVED LODGE
SILAS MARNER
EDITED BY Q. D. LEAVIS

Penguin Masterstudies

Already published:

Subjects

Applied Mathematics
Biology
Geography
Pure Mathematics

Literature

The Mill on the Floss
Persuasion
Vanity Fair
The Wasteland

Chaucer

The Miller's Tale
The Nun's Priest's Tale
The Prologue to The Canterbury Tales

Shakespeare

Hamlet
Othello
A Shakespeare Handbook